EARLY PRAISE FOR WELCOME BACK TO ABUJA ONCE AGAIN:
HOW I BECAME A CITIZEN OF THE WORLD

"Carol Yee has created an opportunity for us to travel and understand the world from our own comfortable perch. Through her travels, she shares the "richness and magic of the ... human condition" and builds our confidence and interest to became a part of our global community."
— **Indira Kaur Ahluwalia, Founder, KAUR Strategies.**

"Carol Yee's book provides a unique glimpse into the importance of overcoming the world's differences to address the global challenges we all face. Carol's career dedicated to fighting global poverty, and a life of lessons, is now available to us all."
— **Kevin X. Murphy, President and Co-Founder, J.E. Austin Associates, Inc.**

"Carol Yee has been an adventurous and curious traveler. Instead of just visiting a location, she chooses to delve into the culture, traditions, and history of her surroundings. Carol gives thought-provoking insights to the reader as she invites them to join her on a journey of global awakening."
— **Debbie Lum, Retired Travel Agent**

"Carol humanizes the traveling experience by reintroducing the "citizen of the world" construct. By offering her own examples of steps taken to prepare for her travels, she adds dimension to breaking down cultural barriers and expanding our personal boundaries."
— **Rockfeler Herisse, Ph.D., Executive/Life Coach**

"Carol makes a compelling case for travel — to destinations both typical and exotic — as a way to cultivate curiosity and understanding, and to counteract fear and distrust, both in ourselves and in the world."
— **Cecily Person, Commercial Banker**

"Carol Yee is a cross-cultural connector and collaborator who brings an analytical eye and a big heart to all her ambitious undertakings."
— **Eric Boyle, Global Development Professional**

"Carol Yee is a seasoned, wise traveler, and her memoir is a powerful meditation on how to become a true citizen of the world."
— **Adam Brookes, author of the *Night Heron* trilogy**

Welcome Back to Abuja Once Again:
How I Became a Citizen of the World

Carol J. Yee

NEW DEGREE PRESS

COPYRIGHT © 2020 CAROL J. YEE

All rights reserved.

WELCOME BACK TO ABUJA ONCE AGAIN:
How I Became a Citizen of the World

ISBN   978-1-63676-592-1 *Paperback*
          978-1-63676-107-7 *Kindle Ebook*
          978-1-63676-108-4 *Ebook*

WELCOME BACK TO ABUJA ONCE AGAIN:

HOW I BECAME A CITIZEN OF THE WORLD

CAROL J. YEE

Explore + Experience!

Carol J. Yee

12.26.2020

Dedicated to my father and mother, Gene and Elaine Yee, who raised me right, and to Susan Puska, who helped me become who I am.

CONTENTS

———

INTRODUCTION

———

Images of Afghanistan often depict women as blue apparitions, totally covered from head to toe in blue fabric with mesh over their faces, gliding down the streets of Afghanistan. But those ghostlike creatures were anything but invisible to me. Who are underneath those burqas, I wondered?

I got the chance to uncover who some of these women were when I worked in Afghanistan on agriculture-related projects in 2004 and 2005.

For one project, I worked in Lashkar Gah, the capital of Helmand Province in southern Afghanistan. Lash, as we called it, is a very conservative city with the Pashtuns dominating, which required me to wear a headscarf whenever I went outside the office or my home. Pashtuns, Afghanistan's largest ethnic group, are governed by the *Pashtunwali* code that requires adherence to certain customs, including hospitality and protection of their guests, family honor, and female relatives.[1]

---

1 *World Directory of Minorities and Indigenous Peoples,* s.v. "Afghanistan: Pashtuns," accessed August 27, 2020.

Many projects funded by the United States Agency for International Development (USAID) and other aid agencies in Afghanistan primarily hire Afghan men for their staff due to the male-dominated society and the lack of educational and work opportunities for women.

This cash-for-work project hired fourteen thousand day laborers to clear clogged canals and irrigation ditches to improve access to water for agricultural crops, as well as to provide an alternative income source from planting and harvesting poppies for opium. The project infused one million dollars a month into the economy of the province. With one hundred Afghan men on staff, we decided to hire a few women to provide opportunities for them to learn and grow. Working in southern Afghanistan presented many challenges, including the daunting task of finding women to hire as most of them remained invisible, hidden away behind the high walls surrounding their family compounds. Occasionally, you would see them walking to the market, but always with a blue or white burqa concealing them.

We put the word out through our Afghan network that we were hiring. On the appointed day, twelve women showed up to be interviewed. None of them spoke English very well, most had not worked in an office, and only a few had worked for non-governmental organizations. We finally selected two so that there wouldn't be a lone female on a project full of men. On their first day at work, they arrived in their burqas, shy and unsure of themselves. Eventually, they became more comfortable—one would remove her burqa and wear a hijab (a head covering) in the office, while the other left her burqa on with the front thrown back so you could see her face.

The Afghan men initially ignored them, but several years later, when one left the project to fulfill her dream of going to medical school, the whole office turned out for her farewell party, with some of the Afghan men almost in tears to see her go. Not only had these women learned their jobs and improved their English, but they also won over the men they had to work with—men who now respected and valued their contributions to the project. When I heard about her send-off from the project, I thought back to my role in impacting the lives and perceptions of the project staff. I reaffirmed that we always need to go beyond how Afghans, especially the men, are portrayed in the media, to discover what they are really like—they are actually like you and me, seeking opportunities to provide for their families. I also realized through this project that I helped Afghan men view women in a more positive light.

But I almost didn't get on the plane. While Afghanistan in 2004 was not as dangerous as it would become, it was still no walk in the park, especially for a woman. Sporadic fighting still occurred throughout the country, including attacks in the capital, Kabul, sometimes targeting foreigners. I didn't have to go, and my mother certainly didn't want me to go, but I volunteered.

Throughout my life, whenever I am afraid, I give myself a pep talk to put aside my fears and concerns, and my curiosity about the world around us wins out and spurs me to travel the world. This is the story of how I overcame my fears to unlock some of the most magical, interesting, and thrilling experiences and people I've ever met.

With the advancement of technology and the global-ization of the world, many more people travel for business, pleasure, or to flee from their current environment. The U.N. World Tourism Organization recorded 1.4 billion interna-tional tourist arrivals in 2018, up 6 percent from the previous year.[2] Travel opens up our minds to differences in others, which can be harnessed to learn and apply what we see in the global arena to our corner of the world. For instance, my experience with Afghan women led me to reevaluate the role of women in the US and how we need to help provide opportunities to all women within our communities. As a result, I developed *pro bono* training in areas such as strategic planning for female leaders of organizations and made an effort to hire women for the small business I co-own.

Some people, however, may not travel much, maybe due to a lack of interest or resources, and so they miss these experiences. Some people think that we should be afraid of people who are different, and that international travel is scary and risky. A 2019 study of Americans by OnePoll for Victorinox found that 40 percent of those questioned had never left the country, and 11 percent had not traveled outside of the state where they were born![3]

I believe that people around the world have the same hopes and aspirations—they want to provide for their families so that they are safe, healthy, and have opportunities to learn and earn a living. I have visited many places where people are struggling to support their families, whether because they face scarce economic opportunities, fighting or dangerous neighborhoods, food shortages, or even poor health. Americans also face some of these challenges. When humans can address these problems of scarcity and conflict, the world becomes a much safer place, allowing people to go

---

2   Molly Blackall, "Global Tourism Hits Record Highs – but Who Goes Where on Holiday?," *The Guardian*, July 1, 2019.

3   Lea Lane, "Percentage of Americans Who Never Traveled beyond the State Where They Were Born? a Surprise," *Forbes*, May 2, 2019.

beyond their personal needs to focus on the planet so that we have a place where we can continue to thrive.

People sometimes view the differences in our cultures and languages as too foreign and strange, which distorts our common, shared humanity. But our commonalities should encourage us to build connections with other human beings and expand our horizons. The best way to grow is to overcome your fears and travel. This can be done incrementally by first traveling from your own living room, then visiting places that seem more familiar, like Europe. Or you can leap to someplace that is different, with different looking people, customs, and food, like Borneo.

I have found that my curiosity and desire to learn about the world far outweighs my fears. My first trip on a plane was from Oakland, California to Orange County, California to visit Disneyland when I was six. I remember getting dressed up for the flight—that was what we did, back in the day—and holding my father's hand as we climbed up the stairs to board the plane. I was anxious, especially since my mother looked terrified during our takeoff and landing. But being with my parents helped to calm me. Plus, I was excited to meet Micky Mouse! I subsequently traveled on many trips, including to China and Italy, with my parents, and currently still travel with my 94-year-old father—Iceland was a recent favorite of his.

In high school, I traveled to Europe without my parents, the first time as a summer foreign exchange student through the Youth for Understanding program and the second on a high school tour. I began to notice that my stomach would hurt after arriving at the airport, an ailment that would plague me for many years. I didn't realize at first, but I was experiencing travel anxiety—me, the girl that loved to travel, getting so anxious about trips that I actually had physical symptoms. The fear of the unknown or not having control over how things might turn out can still provoke some amount of anxiety. Still, I persevered and developed skills to manage my fears, and now I travel internationally for both work and pleasure.

To manage my fears, I developed a preparation framework because I felt travel was essential to increasing my knowledge of the world. I prepare before I depart, reading up on the history, peoples, and culture, watching movies of the place I will visit, and studying the local dos and don'ts. I gather "cheat notes" to take with me, whether it's how to get to my hotel or a place I want to visit; important phone numbers, including the hotel I will stay at; key words in the local language; restaurants I want to try; or even the local tipping protocols. I continue to do this even when I travel domestically. If you develop such a framework, you can overcome your fears and unlock all sorts of awesome experiences.

Eventually, I ended up in the international development field, working on projects funded by USAID. I travel to many far-flung, and sometimes dangerous, places in the world to partner with organizations and strengthen their ability to grow and be sustainable, allowing them to create economic opportunities for their communities. Whenever I go on an assignment, I learn so much from the locals. For vacations, I also travel abroad, as it seems to be in my blood. I am writing this book to share how I overcame my fears to travel the world. Whether it is traveling to Afghanistan and donning a headscarf, arriving in Manila at 11:00 p.m. and wondering if my taxi driver was really going to take me to my hotel, or not understanding the pressures I lived under in Jerusalem until I took myself out of the environment, these were all fears I had to face.

Looking back, I realize that travel shines a spotlight on things I take for granted and provides a feedback loop to illuminate the ingenuity and resilience of people around the world that can be applied to life in the US. Additionally, though I overcame my initial fears about traveling, we travelers still encounter scary moments and situations that require us to manage the fear to power through the crisis at hand. But at the end of the day, rather than be afraid, my curiosity always wins out, and so I travel.

So, what is a "citizen of the world?" To me, a citizen of the world engages comfortably with the world, bridging cultural differences with interest and openness. Anyone can become a citizen of the world, jumping at the chance to get on a plane in search of new experiences. There is no secret password. Being a citizen of the world is a mindset and a journey, not just a destination.

For those of you who have been thinking of traveling overseas, whether on a tour, as an independent traveler, or on a hybrid program, let's take a journey together. Through planning, preparation, and curiosity, you will learn to overcome your doubts and fears to explore the world and unlock experiences and connections to the most incredible humans on the earth.

Not only will I discuss my own travels, but we'll also explore stories that some of my fellow citizens of the world have experienced. We'll find out how I became a citizen of the world, then we will explore language and its differences, talk about differences in food, habits, and customs, highlight differences in culture, religions, and dress, examine assumptions we make about people, delve into technology adaptations, prepare for adverse conditions, and lastly, discuss how to travel from your own living room. Through this, I hope you will become excited about the idea of traveling overseas and you, too, may realize that overseas travel transforms your view of others and our planet.

And what about the title of my book, "Welcome Back to Abuja Once Again?" One time flying in Nigeria from the capital, Abuja, to Lagos, soon after takeoff the plane started to fill with smoke. The pilot calmly announced over the PA system, "There is no need for panic," but that we needed to return to Abuja. As we landed, the pilot again came over the PA system stating, "Welcome back to Abuja once again" before we deplaned to wait for hours before they fixed the plane. To me this clearly demonstrated both the pilot's ability and my own to adjust to reality on the fly. Practicing flexibility, adaptability, and patience while you travel will add to the success of your travels and to becoming a citizen of the world.

CHAPTER 1

MY JOURNEY TO BECOMING A CITIZEN OF THE WORLD

MY HERITAGE

As a little girl, I spent my summers on my grandparents' fruit tree ranch halfway between San Francisco and Sacramento. Oftentimes a vintage World War II jeep would cross the small wooden bridge to their house, seemingly on its own. Suddenly, a small head would peek up over the windshield revealing that it was me driving the jeep, sitting at the very edge of the seat to reach the gas pedal. At nine years old I learned to drive a manual shift vehicle and jumped at the chance to drive off to new adventures on the ranch, perhaps foretelling my future life of travel adventures.

My upbringing and heritage helped shape my interest in all things international. As a Chinese-American born in California, I thought of myself as American but came to appreciate how my Chinese background also colored my view of the world.

Three of my grandparents emigrated from southern China to the United States. My other grandfather was born in Winters, California, in 1900, an unusual event for a Chinese person as few Chinese women lived in the US at that time, and I am not sure why or how my great-grandmother came to the United States. Chinese men out of necessity usually came to the US alone, leaving their families back in China. While many Chinese men came to participate in the California Gold Rush in the mid-1800s and then to work on the building of the Transcontinental Railroad, eventually, they were discriminated against and even lynched by whites.

This led to the Chinese Exclusion Act of 1882—the only time an ethnic group was banned in the US—that codified restrictions on Chinese immigration and remained in place until 1943.[4] The law prohibited all laborers from immigrating to the US, allowing entrance to only certain exempt classes, such as merchants and teachers. These restrictions further limited the number of Chinese women here. In 1920, of 13,920,692 people who immigrated to the US from around the world, with the vast majority coming from Europe, only 43,560, or 0.3%, came from China.[5]

After their parents arranged their marriage, my maternal grandfather, a US citizen, traveled to China to collect his bride in 1922, sight unseen; my grandmother got on a ship with a strange man headed for a strange country. My paternal grandmother, at about the same time, was sold—not an uncommon occurrence for girls from poor families in China

---

4   History, "Chinese Exclusion Act," updated September 13, 2019.

5   US Department of Commerce, US Bureau of the Census, *Historical Census Statistics on the Foreign-born Population of the United States: 1850-1990,* by Campbell Gibson and Emily Lennon, Population Division Working Paper No. 29 (Washington, DC, February 1999).

then—and sent to America to her new husband. Unfortunately, the details of that "transaction" have been lost.

When my grandmothers arrived in the US, they both faced daunting challenges. After they disembarked from their ships, they were taken to the Angel Island Immigration Station in the middle of San Francisco Bay. Unlike Ellis Island in New York, Angel Island detained immigrants for weeks, months, or even years as they were interrogated by US immigration officials. The objective of the detention was to find reasons to exclude new arrivals, not to welcome them as Ellis Island did.[6] My maternal grandmother stayed for two weeks even though she was married to a US citizen. My other grandmother stayed for months and would never speak of her time there.

While I always heard stories of Angel Island, I finally visited the state park in 2008. Only the restored detention barracks remain of the immigration station. The visit overwhelmed me as I tried to imagine my grandmothers and all the other immigrants who came before and after them being detained there when they came to the US to improve their lives. As visitors move into the barracks room, you still find poems in Chinese characters written or carved into the walls representing the despair of those detained and awaiting their fate.

My maternal grandparents and great-grandparents were farmers in California's Suisun Valley. My mother, Elaine Lum Yee, remembered my great-grandmother tottering through the fruit orchards on her bound feet. Considered a sign of beauty, this painful practice—which required breaking the

---

6   "Immigration Station," California Department of Parks and Recreation, accessed August 27, 2020.

arch of the foot of young girls then binding the toes so that they were folded under the foot—continued until the early 20th century. My grandmother escaped this practice only because her mother forbade it; instead, her feet ended up as a size eight.

My paternal grandparents lived in the small farming community of Salinas, known for growing lettuce, where my grandfather ran the local Chinese *tong*, or benevolent association, the *Suey Sing Tong*.

All my grandparents primarily spoke in their own local dialect of Cantonese Chinese, the first language I learned. They also adhered to Chinese traditions, many of which we follow to this day, influenced by Confucianism, Taoism, and Buddhism, which includes ancestor worship and filial piety. My paternal grandmother eventually converted to Christianity, which ended her following of local Chinese traditions.

My parents were born and raised in California. My father, Gene Yee, an avid reader, frequented the public library, which filled his head with a sense of adventure and an encyclopedia of information about far-off lands. Both vividly remember visiting the international exhibits at the Golden Gate International Exposition on Treasure Island situated in San Francisco Bay in 1939 and 1940. My parents met at the University of California, Berkeley, but my father transferred to Idaho State College in Pocatello, Idaho, to attend pharmacy school. When he told my grandmother that he was moving to Idaho, she wanted to know what country that was in! After graduating, my father returned to California to work as a pharmacist, married my mother, and eventually owned his own pharmacies. My mother was a government employee. By the time I came along, they were comfortably settled in

Orinda, an upper-middle class (and predominantly white) bedroom community in San Francisco's East Bay.

My family and I have always faced discrimination and racism growing up in California. Sometimes it was subtle, like being made fun of at school, but other times it was more serious. My parents would show up to look at an apartment for rent, only to find it had suddenly been rented. They also encountered resistance when they tried to buy property in Orinda to build their house, the first Chinese to do so. Later they found out their neighbors had signed a petition against their buying property there, but the man who owned the lot decided to sell it to my parents.

HOW I CAUGHT THE TRAVEL BUG

My father instilled in me a sense of adventure. He never said no when I told him about a trip I wanted to take. After our first trip to Disneyland, my parents and I drove to Idaho to fish for trout and eventually took a six-week cross-country road trip to the East Coast when I was nine. Later we sailed on cruise ships and eventually traveled to Europe, first to Greece, Italy, and France. By the time I reached adulthood, I had traveled to many places and to this day I never turn down an opportunity to travel.

But how did my father become a world traveler? As previously mentioned, he was born in 1926 in Salinas, a small rural town in northern California, of parents who emigrated from China. His father died before he was born, forcing his illiterate mother who knew little English to raise three of her own children and three stepchildren in the six-block Salinas Chinatown. She supported the family through her seasonal work in the local fruit cannery. My father never liked school, probably because he wasn't challenged enough. Instead, he roller skated across the railroad tracks to the Salinas library downtown to read the *World Book* encyclopedia, *National Geographic* magazine, and other books that caught his interest. He also read Tarzan comic books at Gene's Pharmacy (no relation), where he eventually worked doing odd jobs, including checking in the new magazines. To learn about current events, he turned to the *San Francisco Chronicle* and summarized the articles in Cantonese for people at the *tong* clubhouse who didn't know how to read English. The Star Movie Theater brought him images of Beau Geste and the French Foreign Legion riding off to Timbuktu. When he traveled to San Francisco, one hundred miles away, he visited the California Academy of Natural Sciences where he remembers seeing a stuffed dik-dik, a miniature antelope. Many decades later, while on safari in Kenya, he was thrilled to see a real dik-dik.

When I asked him whether he thought he would ever see the places he read about, he said, "I never thought about not going." As we reminisced, I asked about the father he never knew. He said, "My father liked to travel, maybe that's why I like to travel." And even now at ninety-four years old, my father still has the travel bug... "Dad, if someone gave you a plane ticket to travel to Timbuktu tomorrow, would you go?" "Yeah, I would go." He taught me that travel is "interesting because there are different places, things, and people to see."

After my parents retired, they traveled more, taking trips from Europe to the Middle East to China to Africa to South America...to every continent except for Antarctica. My father is always up for an adventure! Like the time he and my mother went hiking in the Alps and when he got in a *service* (a shared taxi) by himself, filled with Palestinians in their black and white keffiyehs, to travel from Jerusalem to visit Bethlehem (no tour bus for him). And most recently, he rode on a snowmobile with me on a glacier in Iceland!

At the same time, my mother helped me to appreciate the local culture, people, and natural environment, and especially good food! She also was always up for an adventure, hiking with my father up to Machu Picchu or with me on a glacier in New Zealand, or sitting on the floor of a yurt to have lunch in Xinjiang, China.

My father liked all the places he traveled to, but he especially mentioned Kenya, the western part of China, and Peru. He originally read about hunting in Africa, but when he visited, he only "shot" the animals with his camera. He went fishing near Mt. Kenya, in the Amazon, and on the north island of New Zealand. He always reads up before a trip, so he knows to go looking for Hami melon in Xinjiang or guinea pig in Peru. Gene loves exploring farmers markets to see what local delicacies he can find. And we have been known to drive miles to a restaurant we've read about just to eat dinner. "Is there anywhere in the world that you haven't gone that you want to go to?" I asked him. "No, I've been just about every place I've wanted to…but," he jokingly said, "I never found Shangri-La."

I learned from my father that anyone can get the spark to want to travel and explore the world, no matter what your beginnings are like. You just need to be curious and adventuresome, and "willing to try different things in different places." Additionally, travel contributes to one's lifelong learning, as my father is a testament to this very day. Even as his travel days wind down, he still avidly reads his *National Geographic* magazine as soon as it arrives and watches all sorts of documentaries on places, food, and animals whenever he can.

GROWING UP IN THE SAN FRANCISCO BAY AREA

Living near San Francisco afforded us the opportunity to explore the world without getting on a plane. We attended international cultural events, such as the Van Gogh exhibit, the Chinese Terracotta Warriors exhibit, and the Bolshoi Ballet. Of course, San Francisco also boasted Chinatown, the Japanese Tea Garden, and Russian Hill (okay, there probably aren't any Russians left there). We also visited several of the Spanish Missions in the area, as well as Fort Ross, founded on the northern California coast by Imperial Russia in the early 1800s.

The Bay Area attracts immigrants from all over the world, with new groups continuing to arrive who are interwoven into the economic and cultural fabric of the region. The immigrants do everything and anything...it's not unusual to see Chinese maintenance workers, postal workers, or cooks and chefs in *hofbraus* (a cafeteria style eatery with carved meats) and Italian restaurants. And in the 1930s, there were even Chinese-American nightclubs, such as the Forbidden City, where Asian singers and dancers performed. It was normal to be introduced to different peoples and cultures.

At Glorietta Elementary School in Orinda, the few non-WASP (White Anglo-Saxon Protestant) students had to discuss our "special" holidays each year: I did Chinese New Year, Skip Hayashi told us about kites during Japanese Boy's Day, and Craig Strang taught us about Hanukkah. We also learned about Switzerland from my favorite third grade teacher, Mrs. Crisp, who had spent her summer there and came back to infuse our year with a sprinkling of Heidi, cows, and lederhosen. We also attended shows, including a live performance of Puccini's opera, *Tosca*, in "the city" as a field trip. I was lucky to be raised this way as I had cousins who grew up in rural California, less than one hundred miles from San Francisco, who did not participate in these same international opportunities. I never knew a time when I wasn't excited to go somewhere or see something different, initially in the San Francisco Bay Area, but then eventually around the world.

I always loved getting on an airplane, from my first trip to Disneyland to my first international trip on a cruise of the Caribbean, and my high school tour through Denmark,

France, Switzerland, and Italy. At Disneyland, I was fascinated by the ride, "It's a Small World," and the French Market Restaurant in the New Orleans Square, which introduced me to New Orleans-style food. When our cruise ship stopped in Trinidad, I remember thinking the Trinidadians I encountered spoke a foreign language, when in fact they spoke Trinidadian English, which was accented English spoken at warp speed! I eventually realized it was not just the airplane ride (which has become less enjoyable these days due to long waits at airports and overcrowding of the planes), but the ability to learn about a new culture and its people, visit new places, and try different foods that piqued my interest and helped me grow as a human being.

As an only child and an introvert, I put aside my fears and shyness to participate in a summer Youth for Understanding exchange program when I was sixteen years old, staying with a family in Zurich, Switzerland, for two months. I chose Switzerland because of the impression Mrs. Crisp had made on me in third grade. I still vividly remember my initial memories of my stay there, from not understanding the first day when my host family asked if I wanted "rocks" in my drink (the parents had been to America before and were used to hearing people ask if they wanted scotch on the rocks) and if I wanted to *douche* (to shower in French, even though they were German speakers), to trying to figure out if the kiosk lady just wrote a "1" or a "7" for the amount I owed her.

Since then, I have been to over sixty countries, some of them multiple times, and I'm not done yet. This book highlights things that I have learned along the way that have changed my life. Without these experiences, I would not be able to appreciate the differences each person brings to the world to make us a global community, as well as to appreciate my own family and community.

OFF TO COLLEGE AND BEYOND

After my freshman year of college, my parents and I took a Pan Am (a now defunct iconic airline) tour to China in 1980, just after China reopened its doors to the US in 1979. As we crossed the border between Hong Kong and China, we entered a world where the farmers had not changed much since my grandmothers left fifty-eight years before. Our Pan Am tour guide, Lawrence MacDonald, spoke fluent Mandarin Chinese, which impressed me. The whole experience led me to change my college focus from pre-pharmacy (I had already spent eighteen years growing up in a pharmacy) to history and studying Mandarin Chinese (my family speaks primarily English at home, with some Cantonese Chinese). Through a UCLA exchange program, I studied Mandarin Chinese at Zhongshan University in Guangzhou, China for two years. In order to further my studies of Mandarin, I "went native," spending most of my free time hanging out with Chinese workers and a Chinese family. When I got off the plane in San Francisco during the summer of my two-year stay, my parents didn't recognize me because I looked like a Chinese girl with pigtails and Mary Jane shoes.

I decided to study for an M.B.A. in International Management from the Monterey Institute of International Studies, as I could not imagine getting a domestically focused job. After moving to the Washington, DC area, I found "international development," a field that I have now worked in for over twenty-five years. I primarily work on foreign assistance projects funded by the United States Agency for International Development (USAID) to provide training and technical assistance, most recently focused on the management systems of organizations, in developing countries. My work allows me to travel all over the world to places I never dreamed I would visit but had often read about: Samarkand in Uzbekistan, the Kremlin in Russia, the Salang Tunnel in Afghanistan, the Island of Mozambique in Mozambique, the Pyramids of Giza in Egypt, and the killing fields of Cambodia. All these places are rich in history and culture, oftentimes serving as a traders' crossroads, and I always try to get as much out of a visit as possible, preparing before I go and seeing as much as I can while there.

From this foundation, I became a citizen of the world, comfortable jetting off to all parts of the globe at the drop of a hat, the product of my genes and upbringing. Not only did my father instill in me the travel bug, he also got my mother to love and appreciate traveling, especially trying local restaurants and frequenting the weekly farmers markets. She would make the travel arrangements and organize everything so that all my father and I had to do was read up on where we were going to, then the three of us would be off on an adventure!

All of this led me to fully subscribe to Jules Verne's view of travel—"Travel enables us to enrich our lives with new experiences, to enjoy and to be educated, to learn respect for foreign cultures, to establish friendships, and above all to contribute to international cooperation and peace throughout the world."[7]

---

7   "8 Jules Verne Quotes about Nature and Travel," *For Reading Addicts* (blog), February 8, 2016, accessed August 27, 2020.

TIS A PUZZLEMENT

The question I often think about is how one becomes a citizen of the world. Is it something in your DNA? Is it something you learn? Is it by happenstance?

Why do some people emigrate to another country? Sometimes they do not have a choice, like refugees fleeing persecution, war, or natural disasters, or people who are trafficked. Other times it's for economic reasons, such as the many Filipina maids I have seen congregating in parks in Hong Kong on Sundays, their only day off from the rich homes where they work. And while some people seek out new opportunities, many people stay put. Why? Even within a country, some people are willing to move, while others stay even though no jobs are available.

My father's interest in the world and his love of travel definitely inspired me to travel, taking it slow initially with domestic trips and then expanding overseas. Without his support and encouragement, I might not have overcome my fears and become passionate about travel.

It is interesting that within a family or community, there are those that love to travel and those that don't. My mother loved to travel, probably because she followed my father, but her brother hates to travel. Tis a puzzlement. Do you have any ideas about why some people catch the travel bug or want to learn about other countries, while others have no interest?

I now invite you to become a citizen of the world, to enjoy the richness and magic of the human experience and our common humanity. Come along on my journey as I recount how I overcame my fears to discover peoples and cultures different from my own, realizing we all contribute to the human story and are more successful together than separate. As a student of the world, I plan to travel to different parts of the world as long as I am physically able, while also taking advantage of cultural opportunities available near my home and enjoying the secrets of traveling from my armchair.

I hope my book will inspire you to travel, meet different people, and create your own stories, whether overseas or in your own communities.

Next up, let's look at language and its differences.

CHAPTER 2

WHAT IS A "PROPOSAL?": LANGUAGE AND ITS DIFFERENCES

———

PETE'S STORY

My memories of Pete Siu, a forty-something Chinese-Canadian and former coworker, always start with images of him in Kabul, dressed in the Afghan outfit for men, the *shalwar kameez*, and setting out to find a quiet space to reflect on the world. He currently lives in Washington, DC, and I consider him one of my most introspective friends, never taking things lightly and always having a different perspective on a situation. Whenever I need a sounding board, I go to Pete.

Growing up in Canada, Pete seemed to have a different experience than I had growing up in the US. While some classmates harassed me for being of Chinese origin, I always felt American. For Pete, who arrived in Canada when he was three months old, "they just assumed that I was from a different culture because I wasn't white. And so, whether I was in fact an immigrant or not, I was certainly treated as an immigrant—with different customs, cultural reference points, and social values." His experience helped him empathize with others who struggle to feel included, and led him to view different people, whether rural versus city, Canadian versus American, or non-Canadian/Americans, as people he wanted to get to know, understand, and treat with respect and authenticity.

Pete first spoke Cantonese and did not learn English until he entered pre-school. With his parents, he continues to speak Cantonese as much as possible, but since they have lived in Canada for so long, Cantonese words have dropped from memory, replaced by the English that is reinforced in everyday life. Their English has evolved to reflect new concepts and modes of thinking while their Cantonese remains frozen and retains the vocabulary of the time when they emigrated from Hong Kong in the late 1970s.

Since college, Pete resides in the US, but takes regular trips abroad. "Typically, when I need to clear my head, I travel and it allows me to reinvent myself. It kind of deconstructs assumptions and my ways of doing things, it allows me to get clarity about my life." And it also provides him with the opportunity to learn about other peoples and cultures.

He goes on to say, "There is something so commonsensical about respecting another person's culture. There shouldn't be this notion that there is a culture that is higher than others, as culture is essentially the norms and ways of doing things people are used to." At the core of any interaction is "respecting everybody's humanity and seeing the value that everybody brings to the table."

While he accepts other cultures, he also does not hesitate to try to instill some new ideas into a situation. When he lived and worked in Afghanistan in the early 2000s on a USAID-funded project, he made it his mission to involve more women in the project's activities. He created a women's coffee group that allowed women a safe space and opportunity to come together to brainstorm new ideas and ways of doing things. He appointed one of his Afghan female staff to lead the group—she eventually left Afghanistan to pursue higher education. Later, Pete was also instrumental in working with me to hire the two female staff that I previously mentioned. Most people would not have taken the time to reach out to women in Afghanistan, but Pete felt this was important.

Pete successfully worked in international development before going back to school and making a career change. He ended up working for a charter school system in Washington, DC, before moving on to work for the District of Columbia (Washington, DC) government, where he managed a team of twenty, composed entirely of African-Americans. During that time, he observed how his team often acted and spoke very differently when white colleagues were around than when it was "just family"—he was privileged to be included as part of that family over time. As he got to know them better, he came to understand that "his team had a more relaxed and natural way of talking and being when at home or among friends who were primarily African-American. However, when outside those spaces, whether it be in offices, stores, or in some other space in which the power or authority was predominantly white, his team often consciously or unconsciously used a different demeanor and speech akin to a second cultural identity."

This led him to reflect on the practice and he realized that though the stakes for him were not as high as his African-American counterparts (for whom a routine interaction at a store, for example, could lead to a deadly intervention with law enforcement), he himself acted differently depending on his environment. For example, when he worked at a predominately white upper-middle class law firm, he needed to speak about subjects he never cared to talk about or didn't know much about, and he would carry himself differently.

But then Pete stated the obvious about those of us who travel widely or insert ourselves into different environments. "I mean it's very second nature to me as someone who's traveled a lot and worked in a lot of different places to change how I speak and conduct myself, to figure out what is the predominant culture of an organization or a place and attempt to modify my actions to try and put people at ease." And indeed, this is what successful citizens of the world practice.

So, after growing up "not being entirely of one culture or another," Pete began "being very deliberate about what culture I was representing, what culture I was given the privilege of entering, and my role in shaping culture at any given time. That made me more interested in cultures," and led him to "observe a lot of interactions and see the basis of culture and social structures and think about how important they were."

While Pete comfortably moves among and between worlds, adapting to the situation in a way that is authentic to himself, he also realizes it's a continuous effort as he encounters new people and situations as he travels through the world. And before each trip, he always prepares his mindset and cultural tools, including getting a sense of the language by studying basic vocabulary of the places he will visit.

LANGUAGES

Thousands of languages populate the world today, a daunting challenge for global travelers. Without the introduction of using another language, basic communications between people is hard enough. Yet, Nelson Mandela pointed out, "If you talk to a man in a language he understands, that goes to his head. If you talk to him in his own language, that goes to his heart."[8]

Unfortunately, I don't live up to Mr. Mandela's standards. Although I travel widely and have studied foreign languages in school, I only speak English fluently and at one time had some amount of fluency in Mandarin Chinese. In fact, I always say I know ten words in ten languages, including *smetana*, the Russian word for sour cream. I have no idea why I know *smetana* since I neither hate nor love sour cream! While I try to use rudimentary foreign words, I often resort to sign language when interacting with foreigners…pointing, miming, or even drawing a picture.

Locals usually appreciate your attempt to speak in their language, except in Paris, where if you pronounce a word even slightly off, they will not understand you. Once in a small Asian takeout restaurant in Paris we realized some mustard would enhance the flavors of our food. The French call mustard *moutarde*, but we could never get the pronunciation right for the servers to understand us, and they did not understand English. The servers did speak Vietnamese, which we did not, although we even tried Cantonese and Mandarin. Alas, nothing worked, and we went without mustard that day.

---

8   "5 Inspiring Quotes for Language Learners," *Telc Language Tests* (blog), January 2016.

You may actually communicate easier with non-native speakers of a language. Or you may find a third language that you both know. An interesting exchange happened in the desert in northwestern China, in the middle of nowhere in the Xinjiang Uyghur Autonomous Region. Susan Puska, my partner and now spouse, and I stopped to see some tombs. A Han Chinese (China's majority ethnic group) came up while we chatted with the Uyghur ticket seller, but he could not understand her heavily accented Chinese. Instead, Susan, used to hearing foreigners speak Chinese, stepped up to interpret between the Han Chinese and the Uyghur. We cracked up at this exchange and the look on his face as we headed towards the region's capital, Urumqi.

Sometimes you get the gist of the conversation from the context, as well as understanding a word here and there. Faking it can also work…I often nod my head when someone speaks to me in a foreign language, acknowledging that they are speaking and encouraging them to continue. Once in France, I impressed Susan as she marveled that I could understand the shopkeeper. Dumbfounding her, I commented, "Oh I don't, but I get the gist of the conversation." Maybe I should have left Susan impressed instead!

Even in the US we face language challenges. In Michigan, they want pop—when I looked around for their father, I didn't find anyone, instead they wanted a soda pop, or soda, as it's called in other parts of the country. And then there are regional accents—the Boston accent, New York accent, the Midwestern twang, the southern drawl. Not only do foreigners struggle with these differences, but so do Americans.

DIFFERENCE IN LANGUAGES

An important element of how we communicate, especially when traveling overseas, focuses on languages. As Americans, we often forget that many parts of the world speak a language other than English. Native English speakers only account for 378 million people, even though it is now the business language of the world.[9] Approximately 1.3 billion people speak Mandarin Chinese as native speakers alone, more than 440 million speak Spanish, over 315 million speak Arabic, over 260 million speak Hindi/Urdu, and less than 100 million speak French.[10] French, once the language of diplomacy from the 17th century until the mid-20th century, diminished in popularity when English supplanted it as the new *lingua franca,* or common language, to use in diplomacy and business.[11]

Some languages include different dialects—sometimes mutually understandable and other times not. While all Arabic speakers use Modern Standard Arabic for written and formal speaking, dialectal Arabic is what people speak normally and differs from country to country.[12] Thus, the pronunciation of Moroccan Arabic differs greatly from Egyptian Arabic, or that of the Persian Gulf. Interestingly, much of the Arabic speaking world understands Egyptian Arabic, as the Egypt film and television industry dominates the Arab world.

---

9   Anil, "English Language Statistics – an Exhaustive List," *Lemon Grad* (blog), accessed August 28, 2020.

10 Nicole, "The 10 Most Common Languages," *Accredited Language Services* (blog), January 9, 2019.

11 T.G. Otte, review of *Satow's Guide to Diplomatic Practice* by Sir Ivor Roberts, ed., *H-Diplo*, September 1, 2010.

12 Randa A., "How Different Are Arabic Dialects." *Eton Institute* (blog), April 15, 2018.

Chinese includes dialects and subdialects, even though the People's Republic of China (PRC) and Taiwan (the Republic of China) designated Mandarin Chinese as their official language. All Chinese dialects use the same written language, although China simplified some of its characters, while Taiwan continues to use the traditional characters. Hong Kong (once a British Colony and now a special administrative region of China) also uses traditional characters, but theirs evolved a bit differently. For example, the Mandarin for "not have" is 沒有 (mei you), with the 有 character meaning "to have." In Hong Kong they developed the character 冇 for "not have" that removes the horizontal lines from 有 meaning "to have" signaling "not have!" Japan and Korea also use traditional Chinese characters within their own writing systems.

Chinese is a tonal language, where the meaning of the word differs depending on what tone is used. Mandarin Chinese has four tones, while Cantonese has six tones (or nine, depending on how you count them).[13] The spoken language includes between seven and ten major dialects, such as Shanghainese, Cantonese, and Fukienese. People speaking one of these dialects often can't communicate with someone speaking another dialect. When confronted with comprehension problems, they sometimes resort to tracing characters on their outstretched palms to get the message across. When people whose first language is a different Chinese dialect speak in Mandarin Chinese, they do so with a regional, often thick, accent. For example, Mao Zedong (or Mao Tse-tung) spoke Mandarin with a thick Hunan accent.[14] Interestingly, when I speak in Mandarin Chinese in China,

---

13   John McWhorter, "The World's Most Musical Languages," *The Atlantic*, November 13, 2015.

14   *New World Encyclopedia*, s.v. "Mao Zedong," accessed August 28, 2020.

although I am neither a native nor fluent speaker, the Chinese immediately can detect I have origins in southern China, even though I can't detect a "southern" accent.

Within these dialects, you also have subdialects. For example, in most parts of Guangdong Province, people speak Cantonese. The word Cantonese comes from the language spoken in the area of Canton, a Portuguese transliteration of Guangdong.[15] Canton now goes by the name Guangzhou, the provincial capital of Guangdong, with "standard" Cantonese centered there. Yet subdialects are found throughout the province.

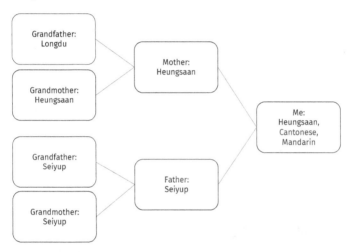

As you see in the above graphic, I exemplify a few of the subdialects found in Guangdong. My maternal grandmother's family originates from the Zhongshan area, fifty miles south of Guangzhou, and the first language I learned was her subdialect, called *Heungsaan* in Cantonese or

---

15   Sara Naumann, "A Short History of Guangzhou," *TripSavvy* (blog), May 16, 2017.

Xiangshan in Mandarin, which is slightly different than that of Guangzhou. My maternal grandfather's family hails from a village near Zhongshan, which speaks another subdialect, *Longdu*, which is unintelligible from *Heungsaan*. My father's family originates from Taishan, seventy miles to the west where they speak *Seiyup* in Cantonese or *Taishanese* in Mandarin. I seldom directly communicated with my paternal grandmother as she spoke *Seiyup* and only a few English words even after she lived in the US for over forty years.

To top it all off, I lived in Guangzhou for two years studying Mandarin Chinese (which my family does not speak at all). I studied at Zhongshan University, where people on campus tended to speak Mandarin, but at home or outside the university they spoke the standard Cantonese version, or *Samyup* in Cantonese. To learn more about the local culture and language in Guangzhou, I hung out with Chinese families as much as possible. My listening skills in Cantonese improved dramatically, but I always hesitated to speak in Cantonese due to the slight differences between the standard version of Cantonese and *Heungsaan*. I never know which subdialect I am speaking, Cantonese or *Heungsaan*, so I tend not to speak at all.

Another situation arises with the Cantonese speakers in the US whose relatives came from China in the early 20th century. My parents and others of their generation first learned Cantonese from their parents, with limited changes to the words they used, while Cantonese in China and Hong Kong continued to evolve, including transliterating English words like "jeep." But the Cantonese of my parents remained static, with English words filling in for new inventions, such as "computer" instead of the Chinese word for computer. As previously mentioned, Pete faces a similar situation when speaking Cantonese with his parents.

So, when my parents and I traveled to China and Hong Kong in 1980, my father ordered *leung sui*, what we called soda pop in the San Francisco Bay Area, in a dim sum restaurant. The waiter disappeared for a long time and when he returned he had a glass of tea. It turned out that in Hong Kong *leung sui* referred to a medicinal tea, while Coca-Cola was transliterated into Cantonese.

Accents differ in other languages too. Spanish is understood by Spanish speakers the world over, but Spanish from Spain sounds different than that from Mexico. And while Portuguese is a different language, many Spanish words are understandable to native Portuguese speakers as both are Romance languages.

As an English speaker, you may find languages with words that include many consonants or different letters a challenge to pronounce. Examples include Icelandic and Finnish. When the Eyjafjallajökull volcano erupted in Iceland in 2010, non-Icelanders could not pronounce the name and resorted to calling it "E15" for the number of letters after the first letter, "E." Meanwhile hyvää päivää in Finnish means good day!

Even when people in another country speak English, potential for misunderstandings abounds. For example, if a British person (or a "Brit," as commonly used in the global setting) says, "that's not bad," a non-Brit might think he means "not great," while what he really means is "that's good." In India, an English-speaking colleague may offer everyone in the office a sweet treat, proudly saying that his daughter passed out. What? She fainted? No, she passed her school exams and will advance to the next grade level!

Not only may you have trouble understanding and being understood by a Brit or an Aussie (Australian) or a Kiwi (New Zealander), can you imagine how difficult non-native English speakers find it to communicate in English? First, did they study British or American English? How proficient are they in English, and can they understand your accent or keep up with your speaking pace? Often non-native speakers read and write a foreign language more adeptly than they speak or listen. Speaking in a different language on the telephone is the most challenging because you cannot get visual cues (seeing your conversation partner's lips or gestures) to help understand his meaning. To increase the chance that you'll be understood, speak slowly, separate words and sentences with a brief pause, and request, "May I ask you to confirm, please, what you heard? I am happy to repeat anything that is unclear."

Lastly, remember that when we read or hear words, each person may interpret them differently, with idioms being especially challenging for foreigners. They may know the words but not understand the meaning or the appropriate time to use them. Once our Chinese tour guide got cut when a glass pane broke after the wind blew a window shut. My mother told him, "You were lucky," meaning he could have been more seriously hurt. This offended him—he misunderstood my mother, thinking she meant he was lucky to get cut. We stopped to explain, and only then did he understand.

When you are the foreigner, you need to be mindful of using idioms and the appropriateness of your words. At the same time, if you hear a foreigner using an idiom inappropriately, give them a pass as they attempt to speak your language.

LEARNING A FOREIGN LANGUAGE

To prepare to travel overseas, should you study a foreign language? American journalist, Flora Lewis said, "Learning another language is not only learning different words for the same things, but learning another way to think about things."[16]

Young people definitely should study one or more foreign languages as they get ready to interact in a more integrated world. For others preparing for an upcoming trip, learn some basic words and phrases, as fluency in a language takes much longer than two weeks. But keep in mind, "because the language centers in the brain are so flexible, learning a second language can develop new areas of your mind and strengthen your brain's natural ability to focus," providing additional benefits to learning another language.[17]

Most locals appreciate your learning some basic words, such as hello, goodbye, please, thank you, my name is..., or I am from.... Keep in mind, many locals also study English, so don't be disappointed if they insist on practicing their English as you try to speak their language. Plenty of books, CDs, and apps can help you study a foreign language. If you buy a book, also try an online translation program to hear how to pronounce the words accurately. While challenging, learning other languages can be fun. It will also impress your family, friends, and coworkers.

While I do follow my own advice to prepare, often shyness (and fear) overcome me when I try to speak a foreign language. Intellectually I do understand the more you try the likelier it will be that you learn more of the language. So, I

---

16   BrainyQuote, "Flora Lewis," accessed August 28, 2020.
17   Luz Palmero, "How Learning a New Language Helps Brain Development," *Whitby* (blog), accessed August 28, 2020.

push myself knowing it shows respect to the people. Others who are not as reticent will just jump right in and try to speak.

For those moving to a foreign country, you should attempt to learn the language. It's best to start before you depart, and then after your arrival, take classes or hire a tutor. Also, immerse yourself in conversations occurring around you, even at work, such as in the staff lunchroom. Join a group, such as a hiking club or dancing class, to meet locals, practice the language, and participate in a hobby. Listen to local television programs or the news to be exposed to the local language. When I lived in East Jerusalem for a year, I hung out in the lunchroom to listen to my Palestinian colleagues' banter in Arabic. I asked a colleague to tutor me in Arabic and watched an Arabic soap opera on TV. (I also watched children's programs in China, which helped my Chinese!) I did not become fluent in Arabic, but I understood a lot more going on around me.

While my mantra is that I speak ten words in ten languages, as I mentioned, I do not know the language of most of the places I travel to. I tend to be able to understand more than I can speak. If I return frequently, I establish a small, basic vocabulary list to use. But I do try to reach out to the local people, to learn from them and communicate in some way, even if only by pointing and smiling.

Here's a way to help you learn ten words in ten languages! You can build your own list, depending on where you are going.

English	Hello	Goodbye	Please	Thank you	You're welcome	Yes	No	Excuse me	How are you?	Fine, and you?
French	Bonjour	Au revoir	S'il vous plaît	Merci	De rien	Oui	Non	Excusez-moi	Comment allez-vous?	Bien, et vous?
Spanish	¡Hola	¡Adiós	Por favor	¡Gracias	¡De nada	Sí	No	Perdón	¿Cómo está?	Bien, ¿Y usted?
German	Guten tag	Auf wiedersehen	Bitte	Danke	Bitte sehr	Ja	Nein	Entschuldigen Sie mich	Wie geht es dir?	Gut, danke
Portuguese	Bom dia	Adeus	Por favor	Obrigado/a	De nada	Sim	Não	Com licença	Como está?	Tudo bem, e você?
Arabic	Marhaba	Ma'a salaama	Min fadlak/fadik	Shukran	'Afwan	Aiwa	La	'Afwan	Kayf haalak/haalik	Bakhiran, wa'an-ta/i?
Russian	Privet	Do svidaniya	Pozhaluysta	Spasibo	Dobro pozhalo-vat'	Da	Nyet	Izvinite	Kak dela	Shtrafa, a vy?
Mandarin Chinese	Nǐ hǎo	Zàijiàn	Qǐng...	Xièxiè	Bù kèqì	Shì	Bù shì	Duìbùqǐ	Nǐ hǎo ma?	Hǎo, nǐ ne?
Japanese	Kon'nichiwa	Sayōnara	Shite kudasai	Arigatō	Dōitashimashite	Hai	Nō	Shitsureishi-mashita	Ogenkidesuka?	Genkidesu, ana-ta wa?
Hindi	Namasté	Namasté	Kr̥payā	Śukriyā	Tumhārā svāgata hai	Hāṁ	Nahīṁ	Kṣamā kareṁ	Āpa kaisē haiṁ?	Ṭhīka hai, aura tuma?

Note: Where there are two forms listed, such as obrigado/a, the first is to be used by a man, while the latter is used by a woman.

FACTOIDS ABOUT WRITING

Through my travels, I have encountered some interesting information about languages, which I thought would be fun to share.

Different languages have different ways of writing. In English and European languages, we write left to right. Arabic, Hebrew, and Urdu are examples of languages that write right to left. Traditionally, Chinese write top to bottom, right to left. Some languages comprise an alphabet, such as English or Arabic, while others like Chinese use ideographs to represent words. Still others, like Korean, use both.

Even those countries that seem to use the same alphabet as English may have some different letters, such as the German "ü," or the "ñ" in Spanish. Some languages use different alphabets, such as Cyrillic, Greek, Hebrew, and Arabic, and different types of writing systems, such as Chinese and Japanese. Some languages are easier to learn and recognize than others. For example, as Russian uses the Cyrillic alphabet, if you learn the letters you can make out some words. On the other hand, each Chinese character represents a word, but sometimes similar portions of a character (called a radical), give you a hint at the meaning. If you understand the hint, then you might guess what the word means.

Chinese	English
木 (mu)	Tree
林 (lin)	Woods with two trees or more
森 (sen)	Forest

As you can see from the above example, these three words all use the "wood" radical (木) as the basis for the word.

FACTOIDS ABOUT NUMBERS

Numbers can also be confusing. For example, Europeans write the "1" and "7" differently. For "17," they write

I first encountered the European "one" in Zurich, Switzerland, during my study abroad program when I was sixteen. Excitedly, I approached a kiosk to buy postcards to send back to my family but had no clue of what the vendor told me they cost. She finally wrote the amount down for me. Of course, it had a "1" in it, so I still didn't know how much to pay. Instead, I held out my money and she picked out how much she needed. While that worked with her, I've also encountered vendors in other parts of the world where I would not be so trusting, so be careful.

In representing large numbers, Americans and British use commas to separate thousands (1,000.00) and a period for a decimal. Europeans use commas instead of decimals when writing out currency. So, they write €450,00 when Americans would write it as €450.00. Other countries use a thin space or a decimal point to separate thousands and use a comma for a decimal (1.000,00). Indians separate the first thousand with a comma, but the second comma denotes one *lakh*, so one hundred thousand is written as 1,00,000.

Another point of confusion. We refer to our numbers as "Arabic numerals," which are actually "Hindu-Arabic" numbers and originated from India. But in Arabic script, they write their numbers completely differently.

"Arabic Numerals"	0	1	2	3	4	5	6	7	8	9
Numbers in Arabic Script	٠	١	٢	٣	٤	٥	٦	٧	٨	٩

HOW DO WE COMMUNICATE?

Interacting with people goes beyond language. The way we communicate with each other also comes into play. This comes through natural respect and cultural intelligence. But it also involves the communication styles of different cultures. Two main types of communication styles exist—direct and indirect. In the West, which tends to represent individualist cultures, we tend to use a direct style, focused on being upfront and saying what we mean.[18] Even within direct cultures, a range exists, from extremely direct Germans to more middle of the road Italians.[19] On the other hand, indirect communicators rarely say what they mean and speak in a much more nuanced manner. Collectivist cultures, especially those in Eastern cultures, tend to be indirect communicators, with Chinese on the far end of the spectrum. Understanding your own culture's communication style and its place on the spectrum as compared to that of other cultures provides you

---

18   AFS, "*Direct & Indirect Communication Styles,*" accessed August 28, 2020.

19   Southeastern University Online Learning, "*Intercultural Communication: High- and Low-Context Cultures,*" August 18, 2016.

with tools to better communicate and interact with others as you travel.

WHAT DO I REALLY MEAN?

While this section raises some business examples, any travelers overseas, including tourists, may find themselves in a situation where misunderstandings arise because of differences in understanding particular words or phrases. I'll also discuss other fun facts about certain words.

What is a "proposal?" In my business of international development, we respond to requests for proposals (RFPs) from our clients. In the past, we usually responded by sending multiple copies of the proposal. Often, we would send someone to "hand-carry" the proposal to the delivery point overseas. I used to volunteer to do this so that I could jump on a plane and visit somewhere new, until I realized that these trips elevated my stress level. Would the flight attendant allow me to carry all of the copies on the plane or would he require me to check my bag? Would I make my connection? I decided to stop volunteering for this special assignment, the price of stress not worth a new place to visit.

Once a colleague and I traveled to Afghanistan to carry out a short-term assignment. At the same time, my company needed someone to hand-carry a proposal to Kathmandu, Nepal. My colleague volunteered to first fly to Nepal to drop off the proposal, then we met up in Dubai for the flight to Kabul. When we arrived, our Afghan colleagues asked about our trip, and they found out that my colleague, who is Bangladeshi-American, had first stopped in Nepal to drop off a proposal. Only days later did we find out that the Afghans all thought she went to Nepal to agree to a marriage proposal, which is what a "proposal" means in South Asia!

Here are other examples of when we use the same words, but with different meanings.

British "chip"	=	American French fry
America "chip" (potato chip)	=	British "crisp"

The Brits are well-known for speaking in "code," with books available to help translate between American and British English. A couple of examples include the following:[20]

Brits say:	"I hear what you say."
Non-Brits think they mean:	"He accepts my point of view."
What the Brits really mean:	"I disagree and do not want to discuss it further."

Brits say:	"Could we consider some other options?"
Non-Brits think they mean:	"They have not yet decided."
What the Brits really mean:	"I don't like your idea."

Other examples, especially in Asia, where the concept of losing "face," or being humiliated, prevails, demonstrate that what appears to mean "yes" actually means "no." So, you ask your counterpart to set up an important meeting with his boss. He then says something like, "If everything proceeds as planned…". This could be a subtle hint that it "Ain't going

---

20 Victoria Richards, "Chart Shows 'What the British Say, What They Really Mean, and What Others Understand'," *Independent*, November 11, 2015.

to happen," but he will never be able to directly tell you "no," and pressing for clarification could be bad form, depending on the person and culture. Or an Asian person will lose face if someone in the West points out something wrong, as it will cause embarrassment for the Asian person.[21]

And if you ask a Chinese person how they found something—for example, "How was the baseball game we took you to?"—often they will respond with "*hen you yi si* (很有意思)." Literally, this means "It was very interesting," but they really mean they didn't like the game.

Be careful with the word "invite" when used with non-native English speakers. Americans use the term "invite" loosely, but in many parts of the world, such as China, "invite" means something very specific. If you "invite" a person to dinner in China, the Chinese assume that means you will be paying for the meal, whereas in America you may just want them to go to dinner with you with each person paying their own way.

Some other miscommunications with common American words include the following:

	In the U.S.	In Other Countries
Tortilla	A flatbread made from corn or wheat, from Latin America	Spain – a potato based omelet
Latte	Espresso with steamed milk	Italy – milk
Boot	A type of shoe	Britain – the trunk of a car
Bloody	A descriptive state when blood is all over	Britain – a swear word

---

21 Greg Rodgers, "Saving Face and Losing Face," *TripSavvy* (blog), February 26, 2020.

	In the U.S.	In Other Countries
Bonnet	A hat	Britain – the hood of a car
Barbie	Popular children's doll made by Mattel	Australia – barbecue
Expired	Past the due date	India – died, dead

At the same time, you have instances where, due to language differences, people may pronounce a letter differently than what is written in English. For example, Spanish speakers mix up "b" and "v" as they are pronounced the same in Spanish. When you are in Russian speaking countries and want to reconfirm your Lufthansa flight, the person you are speaking to keeps pronouncing it "Luftgansa," which threw me for a loop the first time I heard this.

Interestingly, we think of a lot of words as English, but their roots are from elsewhere. Some of them we don't even think of as having foreign origin, such as "appetite" from French, while some maintain their "foreignness" even though it is now considered an English word, such as *avant garde*. Other examples include:

Word	Original Language	Meaning
Cheetah	Sanskrit	Uniquely marked
Chit	Hindi	A letter or note
Gung ho	Chinese	Work together
Halt	German	Stop
Hip	Wolof, a language of Senegal, the Gambia and Mauritania	One with eyes open
Julep	Arabic	Syrupy drink
Ketchup	Hokkien Chinese	Tomato Sauce

Word	Original Language	Meaning
Lilac	Persian	Bluish
Pundit	Sanskrit	A learned scholar or priest
Safari	Arabic	Journey
Shawl	Urdu and Persian	A strip of cloth
Tattoo	Samoan	A permanent picture drawn with ink on your skin
Typhoon	Cantonese Chinese	Cyclonic storm
Zenith	Arabic	Top of the path

Lastly, take care to not inadvertently use a swear word, something that doesn't make sense, or that means something you don't want to bring up in a conversation, a tricky endeavor when dealing with people from different cultures and languages.[22] Sometimes, it can't be helped; for example, if someone's name in one language is a swear word in another language.[23]

PEOPLE NAMES

In addition to a few names being a swear word in another language, the names of people can be tricky. In Western culture, we list the given name and then the surname. In most Spanish-speaking countries, a person normally uses two surnames, the first surname for the father's family and the second surname for the mother's family. Address that person by using the first surname or both surnames.

---

22 Chris Ciolli, "10 English Words with Unfortunate Meanings in Other Languages," *AFAR*, February 2, 2017.

23 Christine-Marie Liwag Dixon, "Baby Names That Mean Something Totally Inappropriate in Another Language," *The List* (blog), updated April 22, 2020.

Difficulties with pronunciation and differences in surnames arise when we get beyond the Romance languages. For example, most Americans find the Polish name "Włodzimierz Malinowski" difficult to pronounce. But additionally, Polish surnames, as is often the case in other Slavic countries, change depending on the gender of the person. So, brother, Malinowski, and sister, Malinowska, come from the same family.

Since Arabic speaking countries use Arabic letters, names transliterated into English letters can differ. For example, you can find Muhammad, Mohammad, Mohammed, or Muhammed all for the same name but transliterated differently by people, or even the same person, as they know how to write the Arabic script, but they don't care about the transliteration. This makes it difficult when trying to keep personnel records consistent for your company or to conduct research on someone.

In Afghanistan, many people only go by one name. When Abdullah became Foreign Minister of Afghanistan in 2001, many non-Afghans had a hard time dealing with no surname, so he eventually became known as Abdullah Abdullah.

East Asian names list the surname first and then the given name. The current Chinese president's name, Xi Jinping, is three characters and includes surname Xi and given name Jinping. Some Chinese names only have two characters, such as Lei Feng—this gets confusing because sometimes in the West the Chinese name may already follow Western convention, or maybe not. So, you ponder whether the surname is Lei or Feng. Researchers or readers find this challenging when looking for books by Chinese authors with only two names.

My mother's family faced a name problem. When my great-grandfather came to the US and passed through immigration, the official asked what his name was—he said Lum Foon. The official wrote down his given name as Lum and surname as Foon, when in fact he had said it the Chinese way (the normal way in his mind), with his surname as Lum and his given name as Foon. Subsequently, his children (including my grandfather) went by the surname Foon. Annoyed by this, my grandfather changed his children's surname back to their original surname, Lum, even though my mother's cousins, as well as their offspring, still go by Foon.

"Paper names" arose in the first half of the 20th century, another phenomenon experienced by some Chinese. As mentioned in Chapter 1, the Chinese Exclusion Act, which lasted from 1882 to 1943, limited the number and type of Chinese who could enter the US. Unless you had a relative who had officially been granted entry, such as a diplomat or businessman, it was difficult to enter the US. It was also difficult to reenter to the US if a non-US citizen left and tried to return. So, a lucrative business developed selling "paper names" stating that you were so-and-so's brother, for example. The "paper name" differed from your own surname; to this day, some Chinese families continue to use the name their relative bought and immigrated with, rather than their actual family name.[24]

GEOGRAPHIC NAMES

Going beyond people names, there can also be challenges with names of places. Transliteration systems provide an

---

24   Hansi Lo Wang, "Chinese-American Descendants Uncover Forged Family Histories," *CODE SW!TCH*, NPR, December 17, 2013.

added complication with Chinese. The PRC uses one system, Pinyin (*guo* for country), while in Taiwan they use Wade-Giles (*kuo* for country), even though both places speak Mandarin Chinese. Taiwan even has its own separate transliteration system, colloquially called Bopomofo, using symbols, not English letters, to represent specific sounds. In Hong Kong, which traditionally speaks Cantonese, they usually transliterate words into Cantonese (*gok* for country) and not Mandarin. And if you study Chinese characters, in China they use a simplified form of the Chinese character (国 for country), while in Taiwan, Hong Kong, Japan, and Korea, they use the traditional long form (國). Note that although Japan and Korea developed their own writing system, they sometimes still use Chinese characters.

When going to a country, it is important to know the official name of the country. You don't want to mix up the People's Republic of China and the Republic of China, which has happened on occasion with state visits, such as a 2017 official transcript of a meeting between President Trump and President Xi Jinping.[25] You also want to know how to call the people of the country, and other related words.

I often hear the people of Afghanistan called "Afghanis," but this is their currency, not the people, who are referred to as Afghans. Using the correct terminology demonstrates your astuteness and knowledge of their country.

You will also hear a lot of people refer to Africa as a country, but Africa is a continent that contains fifty-four countries. Africa is often divided up in two basic ways:

25 Gregory Korte, "One-China Policy Gone Awry: White House Identifies XI as President of Wrong Country," *USA Today*, updated July 9, 2017.

- North Africa and Sub-Saharan Africa
- North Africa, West Africa, East Africa, Central Africa, and Southern Africa (which is broader than the specific country of South Africa)

The main ways to refer to the different regions of Asia are:

- East Asia
- Northeast Asia
- Southeast Asia
- South Asia
- Southwest Asia
- Central Asia

And what about those countries or cities whose names have changed? In December 1991, the Union of Soviet Socialist Republics (the USSR) collapsed and the US recognized twelve independent republics and eventually established diplomatic relations with them, including: Russia, Ukraine, Belarus, Kazakhstan, Armenia, Kyrgyzstan, Uzbekistan, Moldova, Azerbaijan, Turkmenistan, Tajikistan, and Georgia.[26] Earlier in 1991, the three Baltic countries of Estonia, Latvia, and Lithuania had already declared independence from the USSR.[27] While not a common occurrence, this creation of new countries has happened in places like Germany (previously East Germany and West Germany), Czechoslovakia (split into the Czech Republic and Slovakia), and Sudan (split into Sudan and South Sudan). In other places,

---

26 US Department of State, Office of the Historian. *The Collapse of the Soviet Union.* Accessed August 28, 2020.

27 Lewis Siegelbaum, "Baltic Independence," *Seventeen Moments in Soviet History* (blog), accessed September 8, 2020.

a country decides to change its name, for example, when Burma changed to Myanmar. City names can also change. In India, Bombay is now Mumbai and Calcutta is now Kolkata.[28]

Should you use the term "mainland" China? While in vogue previously, especially during the Cold War, currently, this does not refer to the "political" entity of China *per se*, but rather to the geographic entity. So, when in Hong Kong, you will hear China referred to as "the mainland" to differentiate it geographically from Hong Kong. You should never formally refer to China as "mainland China" if you want to show you understand the political situation.

WRAP-UP

People often find communications in general difficult—both to communicate effectively and to be understood. When you add in different languages and cultures, the communication challenges increase exponentially. One needs to prepare as much as possible and then be attentive to both the non-verbal and verbal cues, as well as stay attuned to the fact that languages continue to change.

Once during a long layover at Paris' Charles de Gaulle Airport, I rode the train into the city to have lunch. I ordered steak and *frites* but realized that I didn't know how to say "medium rare" in French, the only way I like my steak. I struggled to communicate with the waiter, who only spoke French. Smartphones with their handy translator apps hadn't been invented yet. I tried this way and that until the only thing I could think of to say was *rouge* or red. Happily, my steak came out pretty much the way I wanted it. But to be on

---

28 Durga M. Sengupta, "25 Indian Cities That Changed Their Names and What They Mean Now," *ScoopWhoop* (blog), November 11, 2014.

the safe side, the next time I met up with a French speaking friend, I asked him to write down the right word (*saignant* for medium rare or *a point* for medium), which I carry in a notebook so I don't have to worry about getting a well-done steak in Paris. Later, I also got it in Italian, just in case.

You communicate as best as possible. Sometimes you have breakthroughs, other times you don't (we never got the mustard), but sometimes you end up with a better tasting ice cream than you were originally going to order. You never know, you can just try!

Next up, let's talk about food, my favorite subject!

CHAPTER 3

BRINGING A CANNED AMERICAN HAM TO TUSCANY: DIFFERENCES IN FOOD, HABITS, AND CUSTOMS

———

NICOLE'S STORY

As an African-American growing up in Baltimore, Maryland, Nicole Lowery basically interacted with two cultures until high school: Blacks and whites. The white world also included a large Jewish community, with its different customs and foods. From that background, how did she become a citizen of the world, readily getting on a plane to jet off to all parts of the world?

Early on, Nicole's parents introduced her to different foods: "My mom used to have a lot of fancy business lunches and she would always bring a little bit home for me to taste." Her father, who served in Vietnam while in the Army and traveled to places like Japan and South Korea, had introduced her to things like Thai food and Chinese dim sum.

Her first foray overseas came with an eighth grade school trip to Greece, followed by a school trip to the United Kingdom (UK), France, and Amsterdam. Nicole went on to attend Phillips Academy Andover, in Massachusetts, with students from all over the world. This led her to a career supporting US foreign assistance programs, including a year-long internship in Kenya and two years working on a USAID-funded project in Kosovo. Whenever she can, she takes advantage of long weekends and cheap airfares to fly to places like Singapore or Norway. It seems I can only keep track of her through her Facebook posts.

Throughout her career, there have been two constants for Nicole—her love for trying new foods and the reactions she gets as an African-American woman traveling the world.

Her love for all different types of food clearly comes through whether you are dining with her or looking at her Instagram photos. Nicole loves to explore ethnic restaurants, take international cooking classes, and incorporate ingredients from around the world into her cooking. She even organizes trips abroad around food, like a trip she is planning to the Republic of Georgia. For restaurant recommendations or where to get the best produce, I go to Nicole.

She and I agree that food is an accessible gateway into a different culture. Her advice, "Try the food that the locals are eating." And to encourage domestically focused people to broaden their horizons, she says, "I tell people to try it through food, try out a restaurant or different cuisines as a way to check out something. The next time you're at an ethnic restaurant just order a little appetizer or a snack. If you like it, great, if you don't, you haven't spent a lot of money."

Nicole's love of travel has not dampened despite how some people react to her skin color. "In some cases, you realize these people may have never seen a Black woman before or some people are just curious, but there are some who are rude." When I asked how she deals with this, she stated, "I've become more comfortable with addressing it when I feel that it is not innocent." Additionally, she has "become better about not internalizing that and letting it make me feel a certain way." But she also encountered better cross-cultural experiences than she could ever imagine in such places as the Russian Far East and Pakistan, of all places!

Today Nicole completely immerses herself in a global environment and tries to maintain a flexible perspective. Even in the US, she must carefully plot out a cross-country drive, not just for safety reasons as a woman, but as a Black woman. Despite these realities, she realizes, "I think mostly that people are people and a product of wherever they are from and I try not to be an ugly American." Being "respectful of other people's customs and treating people the way you want to be treated" she adds, "can bridge differences." These are good words to remember that I also endorse, as we face challenges in our global environment, both at home and abroad.

So, let's embark on a food journey, one of my (and Nicole's) favorite topics.

WHY I TRAVEL...FOR THE FOOD!
I wholeheartedly subscribe to American food writer M.F.K. Fisher's quote, "First we eat, then we do everything else."[29]

---

29 Julie R. Thomson, "The Most Famous and Greatest Food Quotes of All Time," *HuffPost*, updated December 6, 2017.

Traveling allows me to do just that, to experience new foods (first) and then new cultures. I try not to eat at American restaurants while abroad, but it doesn't mean I won't have a burger along the way. Some call me a "foodie," but I draw the line on some things...no innards for me, nor do I follow elite chefs. I have not dined at some famous restaurants in the Washington, DC area because I tend to focus on good food in homey places, not the name. I seek out recommendations from locals, especially the hole in the wall places that they love to frequent. On my first night visiting Susan in Nanjing, China, in the late 1980s, she took me to a little outdoor restaurant in a narrow alley with a tent covering for a roof and a single bare bulb for light that served the best soup noodles. The foreign students from the neighboring Hopkins-Nanjing Center sat at round tables next to the Chinese, all happily slurping their noodles.

I also appreciate fine dining, though, including a ten course Chinese banquet or the occasional Michelin star restaurant. The first Michelin star restaurant I ate at was L'Auberge de l'Ill in Alsace, France—everything tasted wonderful! Still, I prefer the local places, like the small, steam filled room I found when I walked into a restaurant in Almaty, Kazakhstan, with only Kazakh patrons and a smiling *babushka* welcoming me with a plate of *pelmeni* (Russian dumplings); I was in heaven. Our common language was good food.

Recently, I discovered other ways to experience food overseas. What better way to interact with locals than by signing up for a cooking class? We learned how to make hand rolled *pici* pasta at the Tuscan farmhouse we stayed at during our last visit. And when in Reykjavik, Iceland, we signed up for a walking food tour with stops at six different restaurants, allowing us to try a curated menu of Icelandic food, including rye ice cream. We look forward to other culinary classes and tours in the future.

Travelers run the gamut on how adventuresome they are with food. Some stick to their hotels and McDonald's, while others sample the *paté*, horsemeat, or *hákarl* (Icelandic fermented shark) at food stands on the side of the road. I suggest you at least leave your hotel and the fast food restaurants behind to try some of the local food and drink to round out your experiences of someplace different. Trying new foods lies at the heart of overseas travel. Here are some suggestions of how to make the most of your experience abroad, as well as what you can do at home, focusing on food and drink.

FOODS FROM AROUND THE WORLD

WHAT YOU CAN FIND AT HOME

With the world's borders shrinking due to increased migration, access to airplanes, and the advent of the internet, it is easier to encounter peoples and cultures from around the world, whether at home or abroad. "Ethnic" restaurants dot the landscape across America now, beyond the ubiquitous Chinese-American restaurant, giving you the opportunity to sample different foods. As Nicole suggested, go to an ethnic restaurant and order an appetizer to try a new type of food as a way to allay your fears of something different.

Those who emigrate from their home countries to other places, known as the diaspora, spread spices and dishes as they migrate, sometimes replicating dishes exactly, while other times adjusting it to the local taste and available ingredients. Although your local ethnic restaurants may not cook the food exactly as you will find in their original countries, even in an international city like Washington, DC, they still introduce you to different flavors.[30]

American journalist Jennifer 8. Lee notes, "What we think of as ethnic food in America may be very different than what is found in the home country, or may not exist at all," as she found when she went to China looking for the origins of General Tso's chicken, commonly found in Chinese-American restaurants, that the Chinese had never heard of the dish.[31] Another example crops up in Indian restaurants that proliferate in the UK, a legacy of the British Empire. But the Northern Ireland Indian restaurants downshifted the spiciness so much that a friend of Indian heritage could not find recognizable Indian food in Belfast.

Another phenomenon occurs when the diaspora keeps cooking dishes from when they left their home country, which may be decades ago, whereas their home country continues to evolve the local cuisine. Pasties in the Upper Peninsula (UP) of Michigan, for example, adopted in the early 1800s from Cornish miners, have maintained a meat and potatoes standard with basic spices (salt and pepper).[32] Yet The Pure Pasty Company, located in Vienna, Virginia, took one of the top prizes in 2018, 2019, and 2020 at the World Pasty Champions held in Cornwall, England, the home of the pasty. Their winning creations, such as a barbecue chicken pasty made with sweet potato, courgette, red pepper, sweetcorn, and pineapple in 2018, shocked the pasty world. This

---

30 Tim Carman and Shelly Tan. "Made in America." *The Washington Post*, October 11, 2019.

31 *TED Taste3 2008*, "Jennifer 8. Lee: The Hunt for General Tso," July 2008, video: 16:15.

32 Erin Wisti, "In Michigan, the Pasty Isn't X-Rated. It's a Portable Pie with History Baked in," *The Salt*, NPR, March 16, 2017.

just goes to show that foods can evolve, and that you may be able to find award winning foreign food right in your backyard.

In the US, you can easily find "foreign foods" to eat, including lo mein, pizza, tacos, gyros, and hummus, all originating from other countries. Foreign chain restaurants also continually pop up in American cities, such as Nando's Peri Peri Chicken, a South African chain based on Mozambican roasted chicken; Paul, a French bakery; Pret a Manger, a British sandwich and coffee shop; Tim Horton's, a Canadian coffee shop; and Pollo Campero, a Guatemalan chicken place. Before Pollo Campero opened in the US, planes coming from Latin America would reek of fried chicken as travelers purchased boxes of it in the airports to bring back to the US. The airlines celebrated when Pollo Campero opened outlets in the US and their passengers could buy the chicken here.[33]

WHAT YOU CAN FIND ABROAD

Sampling local foods enhances the fun of traveling and experiencing the culture and earns the appreciation of the locals for trying their food. It also affords you the opportunity to interact with local people and provides you with stories to tell your family and friends. Interestingly, you soon realize that many parts of the world combine the same basic ingredients in different ways for their dishes: some type of protein, vegetables, and a starch. It's like music...the individual notes can be arranged in many different ways, yet all sound wonderful—or in this case, taste wonderful!

---

33 David Gonzalez, "Guatemala Journal; Fried Chicken Takes Flight, Happily Nesting in US," *The New York Times*, September 20, 2002.

For example, in West Africa, the starch tends to be pounded yam. Not the sweet potato we know in the US, West African yam is a tuber, pounded into bland white balls and eaten with a topping such as chicken stew. Is this not similar to chicken and dumplings?

Speaking of "dumplings," in many parts of the world you find minced meat or vegetables wrapped in some type of dough. A sampling includes: *gyoza* (Japan), *jiaozi* (China), *pelmeni* (Russia), *pierogi* (Central and Eastern Europe), *ravioli* (Italy), *pasty* (Cornwall and the UP), or *empanada* (Latin America and the Philippines). Even a taco is similar; it's just that the sides are not pinched together into a "dumpling."

Many places use spices that may be very different. My friend Laura Gerdsen Widman, whom I went to elementary school with, spent several months in Borneo, Indonesia, on a high school exchange program. She described the country as "beautiful, a feast for the senses, with the colors, the fabrics, and the tastes of the food." She went on to say, "The food was the best I've ever had in my life and you cannot replicate those spices here, I've tried Indonesian restaurants in the US, and nothing compares." Like Laura, I have had incredible meals overseas, whether something quite plain but tasty and fresh, to heavily spiced foods, all delicious!

You do have to be careful about spiciness overseas. Depending on your "spicy" tolerance level, you may want your food "mild" in Thailand, India, or Mozambique. I never expected to eat one of the spiciest meals ever in a hotel near the Rome airport where I was on a forced overnight and given a voucher for dinner. I ordered pasta arrabbiata, a "spicy" pasta dish, and a (tiny, by today's standards) bottle of Coca-Cola. I started eating and thought I would die; it was so hot. The Coke did nothing to stop the burn and I had no *lire* (Italian money at the time) to buy any water (and I was unsure if you could drink the tap water since none of the Italians drank it). I've ordered that same dish in other restaurants with a spice level at a slow burn, so either the chef's hand slipped when he was adding the chili peppers, or the chef didn't know how to cook this dish! Another memorable "too spicy to eat" moment occurred in a Thai restaurant in Hong Kong. Never again will I order "hot" in a Thai restaurant overseas even though I can tolerate "hot" in a Thai restaurant in the US.

Similar to the dumpling, spices differ across the globe, so for example, even though curry usually contains turmeric, coriander, and chilies, the other spices and ingredients added will make the "curry" taste different.[34] In Japan, the curry is on the sweeter side; in Thailand it can be red, green, or yellow and is often made with coconut milk; in India, Punjabi curry in the north is made with ghee (clarified butter) while southern curry is light and liquidy. You can also find curry from South Africa to the UK to the West Indies—perhaps a legacy of British colonialism.[35] Each place will be different, including what type of protein is typical, yet they are all known as curry.

34 "Homemade Curry Powder," *Chili Pepper Madness* (blog), June 19, 2019.
35 "The Story of Curry – and How It Became the UK's National Dish," *UPB* (blog), April 14, 2016.

In many parts of the world (or at least in hotels catering to Westerners), you can order spaghetti bolognese; some of it is more like the Italian way, but in other places it will have local nuances. In Ghana, I stayed at a small, local hotel and ordered spaghetti bolognese—I got a huge plate of pasta with a meat sauce that also contained mixed vegetables, the frozen kind. I ate it as I was hungry, although it was a bit strange. Several years later, I found myself at the same hotel. Forgetting that the spaghetti was strange, I ordered it again. As soon as the server placed it in front of me, I remembered it! Chinese-Americans even serve a form of "spaghetti bolognese" called tomato beef chow mein.

While cheese fondue from Switzerland is vastly different from Chinese hot pot, the Swiss got smart and developed *fondue Chinoise*, which copies the Chinese use of broth as the medium to cook your food instead of cheese. You can also have differences by region. In West Africa, jollof rice, based on rice, tomatoes, and spices, is popular, but it tastes different in Senegal than it does in Ghana, with each country claiming the title for best.

Sometimes, the basic ingredients may be completely different, such as goat or snake or dog. You immediately react with a "no way!" But, you may be invited to a meal where your host orders these delicacies to honor you as the guest (and sometimes they use you as an excuse to order a coveted delicacy they really want to eat if their company is paying for it!). You should at least try a bit of what the host ordered to be polite, and if you really can't bring yourself to do so, at least pretend that you are tasting it by bringing the food close to your mouth.

DIETARY RESTRICTIONS

Vegetarians may have a hard time, although more places may understand vegetarianism now. Even though most places have some sort of vegetables, they could be cooked in animal fat or broth made from meat. The restaurant owner will insist it's vegetarian even when the noodles and vegetables are in chicken broth. Also, some restaurants consider fish dishes vegetarian. Make sure you check with the waiter—you may want to learn a few appropriate words in the local language to convey that you don't eat anything with meat or fish.

Some religions or cultures adhere to dietary restrictions or times where they fast that one should be mindful of, whether you are traveling or hosting people in your home. For example, Hindus don't eat beef, Muslims don't eat pork, and some Jews keep kosher. To keep kosher means to follow Jewish dietary regulations, which includes what types of animals can be eaten, the way animals must be processed and prepared, and the separation of meat products from dairy products, including the pots, plates, and utensils used to cook and eat these two categories of food. Once I ordered chicken paprikash in a Central European restaurant in Jerusalem. I waited in anticipation for my dish only to be very disappointed when I saw the chicken in a reddish, oily sauce. Where was the sour cream that Hungarians include in their sauce? Only then did I realize that the restaurant was kosher so they couldn't mix dairy with meat products. Once I got over the shock, I dug in and enjoyed my meal. Muslims follow a similar ritual, eating halal, which adheres to Islamic dietary laws and focuses on the processing and preparation of meats.

Other things to be aware of include the following. Muslims fast during daylight hours throughout the holy month of Ramadan, which changes each year as it follows the lunar calendar. Jews abstain from wheat during Passover, which occurs in March or April, and wheat products are not for sale in Israel during that time. Some Catholics eat fish on Fridays because they don't eat meat that day.

While these dietary restrictions exist, not all people of these faiths adhere to them, so you need to be attentive to whether you are encountering people or places that observe these practices. For example, during Ramadan, if you want to go out for a meal with someone or invite them over for dinner, they may or may not be fasting, or the restaurant you want to eat at may be closed during the day until the fast is broken. And if you are cooking a meal for someone, you need to know if they have any dietary restrictions.

FINDING THAT PERFECT PLACE TO EAT
Wherever I am, I love to eat with locals in neighborhood restaurants, so I search for these gems by researching and asking for recommendations locally. When they don't have

a menu in English, I communicate in whatever way I can, including pointing to what someone else is eating, which I had to do a lot during a month long stay in Moscow for work. Even in the US I ask locals for recommendations, as they know their town the best. You can find some great ethnic restaurants all over America, such as the Polish restaurant, Legs Inn, in Cross Village, Michigan, or the little Chinese restaurant in Baton Rouge, Louisiana, that served the best stir-fried crawfish over rice!

To prepare for a trip, it's always good to read a guidebook or search the internet to see what food precautions they recommend. If you are like me and love to eat at roadside stands, make sure you purchase something that has been freshly made to ensure you don't get sick, especially if you travel to a hot climate. Unless you see it come straight off the burner, you may want to avoid it—think freshly grilled kabobs or noodles in hot soup. You may even need to be careful at a hotel buffet and avoid any foods that have been sitting around for a long time. Also beware of undercooked seafood, which can transmit hepatitis, and mayonnaise and creamy sauces that provide an excellent breeding ground for bacteria. Note that foodborne problems thrive less when the temperature falls below forty degrees Fahrenheit.[36] Sometimes we don't think about these things when traveling as Americans are spoiled by the strict health safety standards that restaurants and food trucks must follow.

While traveling and exploring new cultures and places is exciting, sometimes you just crave some comfort food. In most places of the world, you can usually find a hamburger,

---

36 Al B. Wagner, Jr., "Food Technology & Processing: Bacterial Food Poisoning," *Texas A&M Agrilife Extension* (blog), accessed August 29, 2020.

a sandwich, Chinese food, pizza, or spaghetti, and even American chain restaurants. You can find a Kenny Rogers Roaster in Nairobi, a Shake Shack in Dubai, or McDonald's all over the world, but the menus may be different—no beef burgers in India (where cows are sacred), no cheeseburgers in Israel (you can't mix meat and dairy if you keep kosher), but you can find rice porridge and fried dough sticks at KFC for breakfast in China (yes, they serve a terrific Chinese breakfast).

When KFC first opened in Beijing, China, in 1987, the first Western fast food restaurant to do so, customers lined up out the door and around the corner, excited to try the Colonel's chicken. The three story, 1,100 square foot restaurant, the largest in the world at that time, sold 2,200 buckets of chicken in the first twenty-four hours. The Chinese at that time saw KFC as "special occasion dining" whereas Americans see it as fast food. It amused Susan to see KFC resort to putting the mashed potatoes in plastic bags when they ran out of containers as a result of the number of Chinese who flocked to try KFC! They have now expanded to over five thousand outlets in China.[37]

DINING ETIQUETTE AND OTHER DIFFERENCES

HOW TO EAT?

So now you've had a peek at some of the ethnic foods available, even here in the US, but as you travel overseas, what about dining etiquette? How is it different? Many countries

---

37   Emily Guzman, "This Month in History: KFC Opens First Restaurant in China," *That's Shanghai* (blog), November 28, 2017.

practice their own unique customs, which could also differ depending on whether you're in a formal or casual setting.

In the US, for right-handers, we tend to eat with the fork in our right hand and then switch the fork to our left while picking up the knife with our right hand to cut the meat, then we switch the fork back to our right hand to eat. Yet Europeans keep the fork in their left hand with the tines facing down and the knife in their right hand and never switch. Why do Americans usually (unless you've adopted the European method) eat differently than Europeans? Americans followed the fashionable French in the 18th century but failed to change in the mid-19th century when the French switched to the current European way. So, what was once in style is now behind the times![38]

Some cultures, such as the Bedouins in the Middle East or rural Muslim communities in Cameroon, eat with their hands. If you are in the Middle East, parts of Africa, and India, you eat with your right hand.[39] You will sometimes be given a bowl to wash your hands in before you eat. For a person who is not used to eating with your hands, it is tricky and awkward to take some *fou fou* (mashed cassava and green plantains) and dip it into groundnut soup and get it all in your mouth without dripping!

East Asian cultures use chopsticks, which can sometimes be a challenge, especially if serving spoons are not provided. Originally, I was a daddy's little girl and tried to copy everything my father did, including learning how to use chopsticks at an early age. Years later, I realized that he did not use

---

38 Aoife McElwain, "Why Don't Americans Know How to Use a Knife and Fork?" *The Irish Times*, March 10, 2018.

39 Amanda Ruggeri, "15 International Food Etiquette Rules That Might Surprise You," *CNN Travel*, February 29, 2012.

chopsticks "properly," like they teach you on the chopstick sleeve at a Chinese-American restaurant, but had devised his own way of using them. As a result, I never had good control of my chopsticks, but that did not matter so much because we used serving spoons to get the food to our plate or bowl.

But, when living in China and visiting peoples' homes for dinner, I left a trail of food from the serving dish to my bowl as I lost bits and pieces along the way since they did not use serving spoons. It was a waste of precious food and it especially embarrassed me as an ethnic Chinese. So, I forced myself to learn how to use chopsticks properly to provide more long-distance control. One important taboo to know when you lay your chopsticks down, you must lay them on the chopstick rest, if provided, or on the edge of your bowl or plate. NEVER stick your chopsticks into the rice in your bowl, which is what is done when making an offering to a dead person.

According to their culture, some Asian cultures do NOT use chopsticks, unless it's with a bowl of noodles. In Thailand, for example, you get a fork and a spoon, but you are supposed to use the fork to shovel food onto your spoon, and then raise the spoon to your mouth. The Thais never put a fork into their mouths.[40] So, when dining in a Thai restaurant, if you think you are savvy to ask for chopsticks, don't! And don't feel indignant if they say they don't have any.

In some parts of the world, you sit on the floor to eat. Examples of this are Japan, Afghanistan, and Palestine. We, as Americans, might find this very awkward as most of us have not developed our muscles in this way and become stiff

---

40 Greg Rodgers, "Table Manners and Food Etiquette in Thailand," *TripSavvy* (blog), updated February 26, 2020.

when sitting on the floor—try to find a comfortable position and imitate your hosts as best as possible.

WHEN TO EAT? AND OTHER FUN TIDBITS

What are people's dining habits? In some places in Europe, traditionally they eat their big meal of the day at lunch, with a smaller snack for dinner. Spaniards take a three-hour lunch with wine and *siesta* (nap) before going back to work late in the afternoon after the temperature starts cooling down. In Italy, they can eat three-hour sit-down lunches as well, but alternatively they visit little cafes where you stand at the bar (counter) and eat a sandwich and drink an espresso—if you take your sandwich and espresso to a table, they will charge you more. In France, everyone eats lunch at 12:00 p.m.[41] In fact, most restaurants only open between 12:00 and 2:00 p.m. for lunch—if you miss this window, you may be able to find a sandwich at a bar, but not much else. Traveling by train in France once, we opened our sandwiches just after 11:00 a.m. as our stomachs growled. The other passengers stared critically at us; promptly at 12:00 p.m. they all opened their sandwiches and ate their lunch. After this embarrassing moment, we remembered to never commit this error again.

The evening meal can be different too. As mentioned in Chapter 1, I lived with a Swiss family for a summer as an exchange student. We ate our main meal at lunch (the entire family came home) and then for dinner we ate bread, cheese, and jam. I never got used to this as my family eats their main meal for dinner. In many parts of Europe, dinner is never eaten at 6:00 p.m.; at the earliest, you might find a restaurant

---

41   Kelby Carr, "Shop, Restaurant, and Museum Hours in France," *TripSavvy* (blog), updated June 11, 2019.

open at 7:00 p.m. (when I travel for work, I often find myself starving as I wait for the hotel dining room to open at 7:00 p.m.!). And in some places, such as in Spain, people often do not eat dinner until 11:00 p.m. or later. So, for my Spanish friend who lives in the US, when we suggest meeting at 7:00 p.m. for dinner (already a concession to her for us to "eat late"), she views it as a late lunch rather than dinner!

In southern Spain one year, we rented a house outside a small town with a park in the middle of the town. One evening we decided to see what was happening at the park. We found a wonderful meeting place there for all the towns-people, a cooler and more friendly place to meet than to stay at home. They milled about, talking and visiting, and watched the children play. One night when we passed by late at 11:00 p.m. (late for us, that is), we found the park full of people, including small children and the old folks. But the best part was that we made a wonderful discovery of freshly cooked prawns and handmade potato chips! Needless to say, we stopped here several times to eat this delicious food and participate in the local, welcoming atmosphere.

At the other extreme, I visited Moscow one November with the weather turning cold, maybe not by Moscow standards, but I already wore silk long underwear, several layers of clothes, and a heavy wool coat. I spent my weekends walking all over the city—Moscow fascinated me with its abundant cupolas on Orthodox churches and the Kremlin rising above the Moskva River. The Muscovites were out and about too, often walking around eating ice cream, which was for sale everywhere in the streets, in the freezing cold! And evidently, they continue to do so throughout the winter. I wondered if other cold climes followed suit or if only the Russians maintained this custom.

In southern China, south of the Yangtze River, traditionally they did not heat the houses during the winter. And while it never got below freezing in Guangzhou, I never warmed up as I sat shivering in my cement dorm room where I lived for two years. In this weather, you will get hot tea when you go to someone's house for dinner, but you will never get hot soup. I found this baffling as I sat there freezing and thinking how a nice bowl of hot soup would warm me. Much to my surprise, I did eventually get a bowl of hot soup—in the middle of summer when it was extremely hot and humid and with no air conditioning to be found. This confused me until they told me why—in the summer you sweat a lot and need to replace your fluids (this is why they don't serve you hot soup in the winter as you don't sweat a lot). Additionally, they serve you hot soup to make you hotter and sweat more, which has a cooling effect on your skin. I have now come to accept this, but it still seems contradictory to me.

Finally, in many cultures, the host continues to pile food onto your plate, no matter how much you have already eaten. So, at some point just stop eating, even though your plate remains full, in order to get him to stop. This happened to me on many occasions in Asia and the Middle East, which is discombobulating since my mother taught me to always clean my plate (as she told me there were starving children in China when I was a kid). In China, especially during a formal banquet, the rice will be brought out towards the end of the meal, but your host will actually not expect you to eat much, if any, of the rice. Instead, he wants you to eat your fill of the dishes with meats, seafood, and vegetables, and only sees rice as an afterthought. If you start eating a lot of rice, he will feel that you did not get enough to eat of the other dishes and will feel bad. And if you are at a banquet in China, the custom is for the eldest, highest-ranking, or guest of honor to start eating first, only then can others begin to eat.[42]

WATER AND ICE

To accompany your food, you need a beverage, which first brings us to the issue of water and ice. Serving ice in drinks is an American custom, even a necessity for many people. Europeans do not use ice, even the Muscovites who love ice cream in the winter would never drink ice water or iced tea! In Europe these days, you may be offered ice because you are an American, but you will only get one or two small cubes. Don't be surprised when you listen in on conversations on a plane back to the US from Europe and hear the sigh of relief as American tourists get served their drinks by the flight attendant and to their delight they find a glass full of ice.

In other places in the world, such as in Africa and Asia, you need to be careful about the ice—check the Centers for Disease Control and Prevention (CDC) for alerts.[43] If you are in a country with an advisory not to drink the tap water, also avoid the ice. Some high-end places geared towards foreign travelers may use clean water to make ice, but other places will use the tap water, a potentially problematic situation you do not want to tempt. In such places, it may be safer to order your drink without ice or a hot drink instead rather than wonder if the ice in a cold drink is safe. If you are at a higher-end place, you can ask the waiter or bartender whether or not they use clean water for the ice.

---

42 Greg Rodgers, "Chinese Table Manners: Basic Dining Etiquette, *TripSavvy* (blog), updated December 22, 2019.

43 Centers for Disease Control and Prevention, *Traveler's Health*, accessed September 3, 2020.

Interestingly, in Cambodia, ice is prevalent and okay to use, a legacy of the French colonization of Indochina. The French instilled a practice of using clean water to make ice to combat the heat and humidity of the area. In the markets, you can buy crushed ice and watch as it's being crushed before you, which you may deem to not be so sanitary. But I always order drinks with ice in Cambodia and have never gotten sick.

Speaking of water, our bodies get used to the water and soil where we live—we build up immunities to the bacteria we encounter, so water in other areas may make us sick.[44] Additionally, in some places of the world, while the water may be clean at its source, it travels through contaminated pipes before it reaches your tap, so the tap water carries waterborne illnesses. Water polluted with chemicals can also be a problem. Read up on the water situation in the places you will visit. The CDC, the internet, or a guidebook will provide good sources of information.

In places where you can't drink the tap water, you will need to decide whether or not to use the tap water to brush your teeth. Some people play it safe and only use bottled water to brush, while others go ahead and use the tap water. I usually use tap water to brush, but when I was in Nepal, the water out of the faucet was brown—a great way to remind me to use bottled water to brush my teeth there!

Any place where there are cautions about the water, you should drink bottled water (or beer!) rather than tap water. Depending on where you are, you may also need to ensure the bottle they bring you is sealed—some places will use a

---

44 Jef Akst, "The Influence of Soil on Immune Health," *The Scientist* (blog), January 8, 2020.

mineral water bottle, but just fill it from the tap. When I first traveled to Albania in the mid-1990s, it was notorious at the time for using tap water in mineral water bottles. They told me the only way to know if the water was safe to drink was to drink bubbly (or "with gas") water. As long as it was carbonated, you knew that it was bottled. Depending on where I travel, I still keep this in mind and tend to order bubbly water.

In Europe, it is typical for restaurants to offer you bottled water, with or without gas, but you have to pay for it. Europeans prefer bottled water, even though their tap water is perfectly fine to drink. This habit started back when their tap water was not safe to drink, but the tradition continues. If you don't want to pay for bottled water at a restaurant, learn how to ask for regular tap water in the local language—usually they will be willing to provide this to you for free (I did not know this when my mouth was on fire from the spicy pasta in Rome!).[45]

When the water is not safe to drink, be careful about raw vegetables and fruits, which can also make you ill. Peel fruits to lessen the problem, but even in nice hotels, raw vegetables can be problematic. Individuals choose how they approach foods based on their risk tolerance level—some people are more sensitive, while others consciously decide to be less careful. I tend to err on the side of caution especially after I got so sick, likely from the grapes that I ate at a Western hotel in Cairo, that I needed a doctor to come to my room, the only time I have had to call a hotel doctor.

Locations above 6,500 feet have decreased atmospheric pressure, which plays havoc with sanitation because the water

---

45   Thomas Moore Devlin, "Why Is Sparkling Water All over Europe?" *Babbel Magazine* (blog), July 27, 2018.

boils at a temperature too low to kill bacteria or parasites.[46] Instead, boil water for longer periods of time or use a pressure cooker to increase the pressure in the pot, but of course you don't know what a restaurant will do. Susan learned this the hard way when she ate a yak burger in Tibet and came home with a colony of unwanted, newfound friends in her intestine.

Some believe that "If I drink beer, I can eat and drink anything." Others will say, "I will eat and drink anything and not worry about it, so I won't get sick." Meanwhile, the risk-averse travelers will only eat something that is hot and just prepared, and drink only carbonated or hot beverages. Where do you fall on this spectrum?

TEA AND COFFEE

Speaking of hot beverages, many places in the world now have espresso bars, whether a well-known chain or a locally grown brand, even in places originally known for tea. But still, people mainly drink tea in many parts of the world, especially in former British colonies like India, Sri Lanka, and Kenya. In East Asia, there are different types of tea, which are almost always drunk without sugar: black tea (fermented), green tea (not fermented), and what is called half black and half green (half fermented teas such as oolong), as well as flower teas.

In China, they have a custom where after they pour your tea, you gently tap your first and second fingers on the table three times to thank the person for the tea. This custom originated when an emperor disguised himself so that he could get a real sense of what was going on in his kingdom.

---

46 Center for Disease Control and Prevention (CDC), *Water, Sanitation, & Hygiene (WASH)-related Emergencies & Outbreaks: Making Water Safe in an Emergency,* last reviewed February 24, 2020.

One day, the disguised emperor poured some tea for his companion, who happened to be his servant. The servant was horrified as he had never been served by the emperor before and would normally kowtow to the emperor. In deference, the only thing the servant could do was tap his fingers on the table to represent himself kowtowing.[47]

In the former British Colonies, people tend to drink tea with sugar and milk. Some Americans also do this in Chinese-American restaurants. The server will comply but think it odd, since as I mentioned above, Chinese people drink their tea black.

When I visited Sri Lanka I learned, to my surprise, that when you buy tea there, your options focus on orange pekoe, or the grading (the quality and condition) of the tea leaves, rather than the tea variety. And many teas for sale in Sri Lanka blend different types of tea leaves to produce well-known mixtures, such as Earl Grey, as compared to China where you tend to purchase a single variety of tea, such as a type of green or oolong tea.

Even though I never drink my tea with sugar, I make an exception in the Middle East, where I drink it with mint and sugar, as the locals do, and they tend to drink it really sweet. I think of it as a hot drink rather than tea. If you are really opposed to sugar in your tea, you may be able to ask for it without sugar.

You can find a Starbucks in many parts of the world now, including at one time in the ancient Forbidden City (the former Chinese imperial palace) in Beijing and even in places like England, traditionally a tea drinking country.

---

47 "Traditional Chinese Tea Etiquette," *Teavivre* (blog), accessed August 29, 2020.

The evolution of coffee-drinking habits occurred even in America, where we went from drinking very weak coffee to ordering a triple-shot with caramel. Speaking of which, my cousin traveled to Italy once and ordered a *latte* thinking she would get her Starbucks latte from back home. Instead, they served her a glass of warm milk—she should have ordered a *café latte*! Another thing to remember, Italians never order cappuccinos after 11:00 a.m. as they find them too filling, while Americans often order a cappuccino to finish off their dinner.[48] If you need a weaker American coffee equivalent at the espresso bar, order an *Americano* where they dilute a shot of espresso with hot water.

In the Middle East, they drink Arabic (sometimes called Turkish, depending on where you are) coffee. They boil finely ground coffee on an open flame with sugar, letting it come to a boil three times. In Uzbekistan, instead of using an open flame, a hotel in the capital Tashkent I was staying at made their Turkish coffee in a rectangular pan filled with hot sand. The coffee is poured directly from the pot into a demitasse cup (there is no lid to the pot) until you get to the bottom "sludge" that is left in the pot. When you order the coffee, they will ask you how sweet you want it—from very sweet to medium (which is what I usually order) to unsweetened, which is really strong and is only usually drunk after a large meal. You need to remember not to drink it down to the last drop, as some of the sludge from the bottom of the coffee pot is now at the bottom of your coffee cup. Just drink the liquid, your mouth will start feeling the thickening of the liquid as you get to the sludge—that's when you should stop

---

48   Sophie-Claire Hoeller, "How to Drink Espresso like an Italian," *Business Insider*, June 12, 2015.

drinking. When people in the Middle East aren't drinking Arabic coffee, then they drink Nescafé (instant coffee) with powdered milk and sugar—I do not know why they go to such extremes.

ALCOHOL

Alcohol can be a tricky thing. Some countries and cultures, mainly Muslim, forbid alcohol. Read up on this before you travel. In Muslim countries, it may be very difficult to find alcohol, but sometimes you can find it in special places for foreigners. Be careful with home-brewed spirits, which can be dangerous. For example, South Koreans were said to brew their own *soju* (a colorless distilled beverage) using embalming fluid! Some Muslims strictly follow these restrictions, while others do not. You need to observe how the people you are with react to a suggestion to go out for drinks or when a waiter brings a wine list. If they seem hesitant, you may want to suggest something else, or if they are a coworker, you may feel that you can ask them. I once was in a restaurant in a hotel in Mozambique, a country with both Muslims and Christians. For foreigners it is difficult to tell who is of which faith. It turns out that Muslims owned the hotel, and when my coworkers ordered beer at dinner, the waiter said that they did not serve alcohol, but that he (the waiter) would go out onto the street and buy beer to bring back for us, which he did.

Albania is another confusing place regarding alcohol. The majority of the country is Muslim, yet their "national" drink is *raki* (or *rakia*), produced by distilling fermented fruit. They drink it from morning to night. When asked why they drink it when they are Muslim, they answered that their form of Islam allows them to drink it.

Each country has its own national drink. Sometimes Americans have heard of it, such as *sake* (rice wine) in Japan, but other times it is new, such as *Maotai* (distilled from fermented sorghum) in China. Be careful with the *Maotai*, which is prominently featured at some point during a formal banquet in China. Your Chinese host will insist you toast them (they say *ganbei!*) but he may have designated someone else to toast on his behalf, or even actually be drinking water instead of *Maotai*. Keep your wits about you as you walk the fine line between being polite (just taking tiny sips) and drinking too much.

CANNED HAMS

So, what about that canned ham? Once a staple in American kitchens, they seem to be a rarity these days, but I guess some people still eat them. Once on an Untours vacation in Italy, we stayed in an apartment at a farmhouse in the heart of Tuscany. If you haven't been to Tuscany before, the scenery is lovely, and people travel there for the food (which is why we were there) and the wine. To me, everything in Tuscany tastes better—the tomatoes, the pasta, the grilled meats, and the desserts. Our apartment had a kitchen, but we liked to go out for lunch and buy local ingredients to cook dinner at home. Other people with Untours did different things—some ate out all the time, some cooked in all the time. We started chatting with our American neighbors, other Untourists staying in another apartment on the property. To our horror, we learned that they had not gone out to eat at all, and in fact they had carried food from the US, including a Dubuque canned ham, to eat during their two-week vacation! They feared they wouldn't be able to find anything good to eat in Italy and wanted to make sure they didn't go hungry.

Obviously, they did not prepare well for this trip and missed out on some wonderful meals.

For the most part, food is better when experienced in the country of origin (okay, Chinese food in China was not good in the early 1980s, only skin and bones when you ordered chicken, but it has vastly improved). While home comfort food is acceptable to eat once in a while as a break, it should be the exception, not the rule. Italy has ham, eggs, and cheese too—why would you lug a canned ham to Italy? Especially when the Italian *prosciutto* or *pancetta* is far superior to a Dubuque ham! And if you find you don't like the local food, you can usually find eggs and bread.

WRAP-UP

I think Virginia Woolf summed it up nicely when she said, "One cannot think well, love well, sleep well, if one has not dined well."[49]

I travel to visit someplace new to learn about the local peoples and cultures, but I travel especially for the food, something I would miss out on if I was too scared to get on a plane. I find some of the best and most memorable foods and meals in hole-in-the wall, family places. Seeking out your own dining experiences as you travel is often part of why people travel. The experience and joy of eating fresh prawns and homemade potato chips in a park in Spain, a *porchetta* (roast pork) sandwich from a van parked on the side of a Tuscan road, or fresh, hand-pulled noodles in China can be just as good as eating at a Michelin 3-star restaurant in Paris. I have driven miles for grilled octopus by the sea in Italy, trekked to a Michelin 1-star dim sum restaurant in Hong Kong, and went miles out of my way for a wonderful cheeseburger in Auburn, California. I never turn down the opportunity to drive for a great meal as long as I'm "close" by.

Next up, let's discuss differences in culture, religion, dress, and ways of doing things.

---

49 Julie R. Thomson, "The Most Famous and Greatest Food Quotes of All Time," *HuffPost*, updated December 6, 2017.

CHAPTER 4

WHERE DID I LEAVE MY BURQA?: DIFFERENCES IN CULTURE, RELIGION, DRESS, AND WAYS OF DOING THINGS

SUSAN'S STORY

My spouse, Susan Puska, comes from a small town in the Upper Peninsula (UP) of Michigan, on the border with Canada. In fact, as a child she thought the Queen of England was her Queen, making her an Anglophile almost from birth. She grew up with a Nordic upbringing as much of her family is Finnish, so she experienced saunas and Finnish coffees with *pulla* (cardamom bread). Fast forward several decades and you find a very internationally savvy citizen of the world who travels at an instant. How did she become this way when others from her area of the country have little desire to travel, even domestically? How did Susan become interested in the world and travel?

International travel seems to have always been in her blood, possibly beginning with the knowledge that her grandfather, who lived with her family at one time, was from Finland. She also credits her interest from the stories she heard from her parents' experiences in World War II. Her father participated in air assaults against the Nazis in North Africa—depicted during a moment of rest in a black and white photo he took of a boy on his donkey—bombing raids from liberated Sicily, and missions from England to Germany as an aerial gunner, including D-Day, which was the Normandy Invasion on June 4, 1944. Her mother, an Army nurse sent to the war in the Philippines in 1945, told stories of experiencing the heat and humidity, seeing starving Filipinos amid the ruins of Manila, and treating wounded and sick soldiers. Susan's memories of her mother's military service were represented in the exotic trinkets her mother brought back, including the colorful hand-carved shoes Susan still displays on her dresser in honor of her mother.

Susan's older brother served in the Army in Vietnam and traveled on leave to Taiwan. While he didn't speak much about his experiences, the mystique of faraway places and military service stuck with her when she chose her career.

Some people join the military and never want to leave home again after they finish their service. Susan's father was like that, and even refused to fly for much of his life after the war. While her mother made a trip to Germany and Scandinavia while Susan was stationed in Germany, she mainly vicariously traveled through Susan's trips abroad, always asking her to bring a little souvenir back.

Susan's international interests continued to grow in school. One summer while in high school she attended a program at the Interlochen Center for the Arts in northern Michigan that included musicians from around the world. At a store near the camp, Susan bought a cherished bookmark from Russia. She later learned that "Riga," which was embroidered into the bookmark, was the capital of Latvia, the home her Latin teacher fled as the Russian army invaded. She won a speech contest sponsored by the Odd Fellows for a trip to the United Nations, which enthralled her, and gave her insight into the Soviet Union when her group had a testy exchange with a Soviet official who derided them and the US. In college, Susan spent almost a year in England on an archaeology dig.

Through the tales her family told as well as her own experiences, Susan caught both the travel bug and the commitment to serve her country, and eventually enlisted in the US Army to see the world, pay off her student loan, and access the GI Bill to further her education, while also following her family into military service. After one year, she received a direct commission to Second Lieutenant. I doubt she imagined where the military would lead her. Germany and South Korea were typical assignments, but she also was stationed in China and in Guantanamo Bay, Cuba (prior to the September 11, 2001 attacks).

Providing for the care and feeding for thirty thousand Cuban and Haitian migrants as a logistician introduced Susan to the challenges of humanitarian assistance needs. And the second half of her career was spent as a China Foreign Area Officer (FAO), advising the US Department of Defense on military-to-military relations with China and other countries when she served in Beijing as the US

Assistant Army Attaché and the US Army Attaché. Living in China in the 1980s taught her a lot about the challenges of living overseas and what it feels like to be "the other"—a blonde in a sea of black-haired Chinese was disorienting. Not only did Chinese people stare at her, they also overcharged her whenever possible because she came from a "rich" country.

Additionally, as an army attaché, she faced challenges dealing with the Chinese military and other foreign militaries of the Beijing attaché corps. In particular, there was a colonel from Iran who wouldn't touch a woman, so he wouldn't shake her hand. She remembers, "The first time he did that to me, I was really taken aback, I found that very difficult and I was a bit angry. Instead, he placed his right hand over his heart, which I ultimately accepted." The US also had difficult relations with the North Koreans. "They were in another world where they couldn't talk to Americans. Yet sometimes they would be at a party where people would try to put us together to see if we could find common ground to talk to each other. I remember being herded into a situation where I had to talk to a North Korean. He was probably more uncomfortable than I was since North Koreans always watched each other, a North Korean could just disappear or end up in a labor camp if they did something wrong, so I talked about the weather."

When asked for advice for someone going overseas, she said, "I think you should prepare as much as you can. But once you get there, it's like your whole plan goes away with contact with a country and people and situations. So, if there is any guidance I'd give, it's to try to keep an open mind and a sense of humor, and if you can, get plenty of rest as you learn to adapt."

So, from a small town in middle America, Susan found her path to become a citizen of the world. To deal with the challenges of interacting with different peoples and cultures when living and working in Germany, China, South Korea, and Guantanamo Bay, Cuba, she used her background in anthropology and her curiosity about the world to learn about these places, allowing her to successfully adapt to the situations she faced.

People around the world have different points of view, dress, and habits, even within a country such as the US. Yet as children's author Stephen Cosgrove says, "Never judge someone by the way he looks or a book by the way it's covered; for inside those tattered pages, there's a lot to be discovered."[50] As travelers, this is good advice as we encountered new peoples.

While there are differences that separate us, there are also human commonalities that bind us. We should not view others suspiciously, instead let's be curious, open, and kind. Let's look now at some of these differences.

DEALING WITH PEOPLE FROM DIFFERENT PARTS OF THE WORLD

With globalization, or the increased interaction of people around the world, prevalent these days, there are many "foreigners" all around the world, even in your hometown.[51] You probably notice that it is not always easy to deal with people who come from different lands (heck, it may even be difficult for you to deal with the guy that comes from a different part of the US). But slowly you will get to know each other and

---

50 Goodreads, "Stephen Cosgrove> Quotes," accessed August 26, 2020.
51 "Effects of Globalization on Migration," UKEssays, November 26, 2018.

learn how to interact, whether in schools, shops, restaurants around town, or in the workplace. You may notice these new-comers might not look you in the eye or give you their opinion when you ask for it, or you may feel they never give you a straight answer. If they are your coworkers, you might need to learn what motivates them (which are often different from your own motivators), how they contribute to meetings, or how they view the concept of time. In these settings, because you are in the US, you probably will build a relationship that may be some type of compromise for both parties and you will become friends, or at least friendly.

But when you go overseas, for travel or work, it gets much more complicated. You are no longer on "common ground"— actually, you are now in their territory and as the foreigner, you need to make accommodations to their way of doing things. A wide variety of factors can impact your relationship and dealings with the people and clients you visit. Especially in business settings but also in some tourist settings, you can find differences in:

- How you approach things—whether directly or indirectly.
- The concept of time—are you from an on-time culture or not, do you delve right into business, or do you take time to build the relationship? In some countries, you may need to spend several days discussing everything except business—this is difficult for many Americans, but if you don't do this, you may lose the business to a firm from another country who knows better how to do business in that country.
- Religion and how that may influence your dealings, including the fact that Muslim countries in the world tend to have a Sunday through Thursday workweek, while

Saturday is the Sabbath for Jews, and many other countries have a Monday through Friday work week.

- How your competitors are approaching the situation—their culture and habits may be closer to that of the client, which will then provide a greater contrast to your sell.

Knowing whether a country deals directly or indirectly will help you understand the culture and impact how successful you are either on a personal or business level. Germans, for example, are known to be efficient, orderly, and to the point, even yelling at you when you have done something wrong. On the other extreme, many Asian cultures, such as the Chinese, often take a very indirect route to communicate—although at the same time you may find them quite blunt when they laugh and tell you how ugly your hat is!

Every country in the world is somewhere on the spectrum between the direct Germans and the indirect Chinese. You may not know exactly how someone is going to act, but if you study and prepare before your trip, and you watch body language and listen to what the person is saying, you will have a better idea of where the person is coming from. Also, being aware of where you yourself are on the spectrum will help you in your interactions with the locals. How you deal with these differences will impact the experience you have in that country.

Learn whether your counterpart comes from a culture where they take time to get to know you, learn about you and your family, before getting down to business, or if they get straight to business. This can make or break a deal.

In countries where religion is an issue and people are of different religious faiths, it is very important to tread lightly as you do not want to make gaffes or create problems for yourself or others. Examples of such places include Jerusalem where you have Christians, Muslims, and Jews, or in India where you have Hindus, Muslims, Christians, Sikhs, as well as other religions. Sometimes you can tell a person's religion from the way they dress or their name, but oftentimes for an American traveling in these places it is difficult to discern, so it is better to be cautious.

You may encounter other differences overseas. In the US, we live in an automated world that has reduced the numbers of laborers we use. Yet in China, which has been changing dramatically over the past four decades, you can still find a very scrawny man pulling an extremely heavy trailer down the street, seemingly without breaking a sweat. Shaking your head, you will look on in amazement at a feat that would require a truck in the US.

Additionally, Americans live in a highly regulated world. For example, we have laws that limit the tonnage a truck can carry or how many people can fit on a bus. In many places in Asia, you will find trucks with twice the load it should carry, and buses not only filled to the gills, but also with a load on top that is almost as tall as the bus itself. It is no use complaining about the dangers of such practices; either get on the bus with everyone else or find a different way to travel.

Don't forget that things aren't always static. Depending on the situation, things can change, so be on your toes and don't make hard and fast assumptions about people.

An important difference that can easily irritate people is the different concepts of time.

YOU WANT IT WHEN?
Different places, even within a country, have different concepts of time. If you are in a fast-paced city, such as New York

City or even Washington, DC, the likelihood that you follow suit is high. When you send an email, you expect almost an instantaneous response, and it is not uncommon to almost be working 24/7. If you go to middle America, the pace of life is much slower. People sit on the porch and have a conversation. When they get off work, they are done for the day. There is not the same sense of urgency as you find in bigger cities.

Certain cultures are known for their view of time.[52] In Latin cultures, you often hear the term *mañana* or "tomorrow." Some cultures never start on time, while others, such as the Germans, are very punctual! I know someone of Cuban origin who was late for her own wedding; she took her time getting ready and chatting with her girlfriends while the groom waited for his bride.

In some parts of the world, it is customary to take a nap, or *siesta*, after lunch, usually to avoid the hottest part of the day. Countries from Spain to Italy to China traditionally take naps. In those countries, expect stores and businesses to be closed for two or more hours in the middle of the day.

Depending where you are traveling to, traffic may need to be taken into consideration, whether for sightseeing or meetings. In a place like Beijing, plan your itinerary so that you stay on one side of the city to sightsee and have lunch, instead of trying to crisscross the city, or give yourself plenty of time when going to a meeting. In Manila, stay near where your meetings are as you will never be able to cross town and make it on time. In places like Thailand, the length of the traffic lights can vary (the traffic police can actually control the length of time the signal is red) and sometimes you can

---

52 Bhaskar Pant, "Different Cultures See Deadlines Differently," *Harvard Business Review,* May 23, 2016.

sit for a half hour. Also, if you happened to miss your turn, you could sit in traffic just to be able to go around to come back to the right place.

Once in Nairobi, I planned to meet a friend for dinner at my hotel. My meeting ended, which was some distance from my hotel on the outskirts of town, and I thought I had plenty of time to make it back for dinner. But as we got closer into town, we just saw wall-to-wall cars, and they were not moving. I remember just sitting in the car in the same spot, watching the clock ticking. Needless to say, I never made it and had to call and cancel dinner as we continued to sit in traffic.

Traffic in Cairo is also chaotic. A friend once likened the traffic to a school of fish, with the fish moving this way and that, but all moving ahead in one direction. One USAID project brought retired volunteer farmers from the US to Cairo to work with Egyptian farmers and housed them in a hotel in downtown Cairo. One volunteer, on his first trip to Egypt, decided to go out and walk around a bit. He stood by the side of the road to wait for a break in the traffic to cross the street. After waiting for fifteen minutes, he returned to his hotel and got a taxi to take him across the street. The trick to crossing the street in Cairo is that you just have to ease yourself out into the road and slowly make your way across. The cars will start going around you, just as fish will swim around an obstacle they encounter.

MALE, FEMALE, OR A "THIRD SEX:" DEALING WITH GENDER ISSUES

You may be familiar with the fact that some countries are male-dominated societies.[53] An example that I am very familiar with is Afghanistan, but you may also encounter these examples in other male-dominated societies. When one thinks of Afghanistan, one thinks of fierce warriors or old men, and then one thinks of a blue sack—the infamous burqa covering the woman—nothing visible about her, not even her eyes.

Foreign men who are in Afghanistan run into a few unfamiliar situations. First of all, they will usually not meet the wife (or wives) of their colleagues. Even if the foreigner is invited to someone's house for a meal, the food will be brought into the room by some male relatives, and only the men will eat together. There's no thanking the wife for a wonderful meal. Additionally, there will be times when a foreign man reaches out to shake an Afghan woman's hand, let's say in a business setting, but she will not be willing to shake his hand. Some women will not touch a man who is not a relative of hers, or it could be that she already washed for prayers and, by touching a non-relative male, she would need to wash again. These are usually the gender events that foreign men encounter in a place like Afghanistan.

For foreign women in Afghanistan, it's a bit different. Depending on where you are and the security environment at the time of your visit, you may need to cover your head with a scarf. I also had the issue of some men not willing to shake my hand, which I initially found insulting, but I soon got used to it. If you stick out your hand to shake but it's clear

---

53   "Global Gender Gap Report 2020," World Economic Forum, 2019.

the man will not shake it, they will usually be apologetic, but sometimes not. In these cases, just retract your hand and move on.

But I also discovered something else in Afghanistan, being that foreign women are actually treated as a "third sex." We can do things no Afghan women can do, like eat with the Afghan men (so in this sense we are treated like men), but we also get to do things that foreign men usually cannot do. We are allowed to see women without their burqas on and, when invited to dinner, we can be taken into the rooms where the women are to be introduced to them (and to tell them what a wonderful meal they cooked).

For women who travel and work internationally, we may run into a good many cultures that are male-dominated. But sometimes the individuals you are dealing with may be more familiar with the West; they may have gone to school in the US or Europe, they may be working for Western organizations, or they may just be more open. On the other hand, you may have to deal with very traditional men, and this can be challenging. Interestingly, in communist (or former communist) countries, you may find more parity between men and women under the tenet that the Communist Party improved women's lives. But while women had more job opportunities under the communist system, only rarely were women given positions of responsibility.[54]

Learning more about a country's culture and politics beforehand helps you better navigate the nuances that you are experiencing. It also may provide you with the information

---

54 Helen Gao, "How Did Women Fare in China's Communist Revolution?," *The New York Times*, September 25, 2017.

of when you can push the envelope, and when you need to be respectful of the other culture.

Sometimes you won't be able to know ahead of time how to react in a particular situation. In general, "foreigners" are often cut some slack as we don't know the local customs. Always approach these situations in a respectful manner, and you will usually be able to fair better. You will need to go with your instinct, but also be mindful of the signals you may be receiving either verbally or through body language. Anything you do that is perceived as offensive, just as would happen in the US, will be looked down upon and the relationship you are trying to build won't get very far. Mistakes are usually forgiven; offenses are not. Call upon your cultural intelligence (CQ) skills to tune into what is correct and what is not.[55]

GEOGRAPHY

Let's now talk geography, which can also be tricky. The British returned Hong Kong to China in 1997 and it is now one of two special administration regions (SARs) as designated by the Chinese government, the other being Macao.[56] Hong Kong currently retains its own currency, and you have to cross a border when moving between China and Hong Kong. As mentioned in Chapter 2, be careful with the reference to "mainland" China, using it only as a geographical reference— mainland China versus Hong Kong, for example—and not a political reference. You also need to remember that there

---

55 "About Cultural Intelligence," Cultural Intelligence Center, accessed August 26, 2020.

56 *Encyclopaedia Britannica Online*, s.v. "Hong Kong," accessed August 26, 2020.

is the People's Republic of China and the Republic of China (which is Taiwan).

The Middle East is complicated too, with Israel being a Jewish state and the other countries in the region being Muslim.[57] Often when we speak of Israel, we do not distinguish and are referring to that part of the Middle East that also includes Palestine, comprised of the West Bank and the Gaza Strip, with Israel dividing these two geographies.[58] The West Bank refers to the area west of the Jordan River that Jordan lost to Israel in the 1967 Six-Day War, which was also when Israel occupied Gaza. Many travelers visit Jerusalem with its many holy sites that are sacred to Christians, Muslims, and Jews.

Due to the political and religious tensions in the region, when you travel to Israel, you need to be careful. Some Muslim countries will not let you enter if they know you have visited Israel. If you enter Israel through Ben Gurion Airport in Tel Aviv, most immigration officers no longer stamp your passport, but if it looks like he will, you can ask him not to and he will usually comply. Some travelers visit Israel and then go on to visit Jordan or sometimes Egypt. The rub is if you cross by land from Israel to Jordan or Egypt, the Jordanian or Egyptian immigration officer will stamp your passport, which will include the border crossing. So other Middle Eastern countries will know that you have been in Israel and may not let you in. If you do happen to get one of these stamps, you can apply for a second passport.

---

57 *Encyclopaedia Britannica Online*, s.v. Israel, accessed August 26, 2020.
58 "Palestine," History, updated October 21, 2019.

CULTURAL NUANCES

As you prepare to travel, you realize there is so much to learn and know. How will you ever manage, especially regarding cultural nuances? Refer to the internet, where you can find information on almost anything. As previously mentioned, if you are respectful and polite to the local people, you don't have to understand all the nuances of a culture, but the more you know, the better perception you will leave with them. Here's a list I've compiled that will help you get a start. It is not exhaustive, but it will get you thinking.

In the Middle East:
- It is very rude to show the soles of your shoes at someone, and even crossing your legs can be problematic, as it is very easy for you to unconsciously expose your sole—try it sometime, it's almost impossible to keep your soles from being exposed at some point.
- If you are eating with your hands, never use your left hand, as the left hand is seen as unclean.
- Dress modestly. Women especially should not wear short sleeves or shorts, and in some places, you will need a head scarf or other covering.

In Asia:
- In China, never give a knife or scissors as a gift—they symbolize the severing of the relationship.
- In India, don't give gifts made from leather, as many Indians are Hindus who consider cows sacred.
- Accept or give business cards and presents using both hands.

In Africa:
- Some people in Africa are Muslim and will follow Muslim customs and practices.
- Don't use your left hand to present a gift.

In Europe:
- People are more formal and tend not to call people by their first names; rather, they will call Bob Smith, Mr. Smith.
- Some countries are more punctual than others, so do your research.

In Latin America:
- The concept of space is much different than ours—they tend to stand much closer together than Americans do.
- Remember that the Spanish spoken in different parts of Latin America may differ, and that Brazil speaks Portuguese.

Colors are also something to keep in mind.[59] A particular color can connote different things in different cultures. Red can mean danger in some cultures (the US and the Middle East), while in others it means good luck (China). On the other hand, white symbolizes purity for some (the West), but death and mourning for others (the East).

One needs to be careful about gestures as well.[60] What it means in your culture may be totally different in another culture; it could even be offensive. The "A-Okay" gesture when

---

59 Richard Brooks, "Colours and Their Meanings around the World," *The Language Blog, K-International,* December 21, 2016.

60 "15 Hand Gestures That Have Different Meanings Overseas," *Bright Side* (blog), accessed August 26, 2020.

the index finger touches your thumb in a circle with the rest of your fingers sticking out means "good" in America, "zero" in France, "money" in Japan, and an insult in parts of Greece. The "thumbs up" is similar; in America it means "good," in France it is the number one when you start to count with your fingers, and in parts of Greece it is offensive.

In China, they hold out their hand parallel to the ground, then move the fingers to a ninety-degree angle, with a back and forth motion. The first time I saw this, I did not know if they were beckoning me or if they were shooing me away. They were actually telling me to come in; I was so confused!

RELIGION

Above, I touched on the subject of religion. Religion is a challenging topic, whether or not you are religious. Many parts of the world view religion as a very sensitive topic, so it may come up time and time again as you travel. In Jerusalem, a holy place for Christians, Jews, and Muslims, people will ask which of the three religions you adhere to—they are dumbfounded and unaccepting of an answer that is "none of these" or "I don't have a religion" or "I am Hindu." Some non-practicing people decide to pick one of these religions just to get the questioner off their backs.

Whatever your religious affiliation, tread lightly in this area unless you know very well the religious issues of the region you are visiting. I know an American who is Muslim who argued with the "religious police" when she lived in Saudi Arabia—I don't recommend this for most Americans, but she understood the Koran and what she could push back on when the "religious police" stopped her. A sampling of the hot spots of the world include:

- The Israeli-Palestinian conflict in Israel, the West Bank, and Gaza, with different Christian sects and some of their issues cropping up as well.
- The conflict between Christians and Muslims in Nigeria, especially northern Nigeria.
- The conflict between India and Pakistan, which is partially political, but partially religious.
- The Muslim Rohingya issue in predominantly Buddhist Myanmar.
- Periodic clashes between Muslims and Christians in various parts of Europe.
- The Chechen (predominantly Muslim) conflict with Russia.
- Christian and Muslim conflicts in Lebanon.
- The Communist Party versus Christians and the *Fa Lun Gong* in China.

It's best not to bring up religion as you travel. You can still attend services, visit places of worship, and ask about the local religion, but don't provoke religious conversations. Be mindful that you are a guest in another country, so be courteous and respectful.

TIME, DATES, AND MEASUREMENTS

As you travel overseas, time, dates, and measurements become important, as a number of differences exist compared to the American systems. Greenwich Mean Time is where time zones start. Directly on the other side of the world is the International Date Line, which starts a new day. A handy website to bookmark is The World Clock – Worldwide that has all of the world's time zones listed; it is especially a must if you are traveling to multiple places on the same trip.[61]

In China, they only have one time zone, Beijing time, even though the country covers five time zones. This means that at 7:00 a.m. (or 0700) in Beijing, it is bright and sunny, but in Urumqi, the capital of the Xinjiang Uyghur Autonomous Region in China's far northwest, 7:00 a.m. Beijing time means it is pitch dark. Urumqi has unofficially come up with its own time to make it more palatable, but officially they are on Beijing time. When in Xinjiang, make sure you confirm what time your meeting will be (Beijing or Urumqi time) to avoid confusion.

Additionally, many countries use what we call "military time," which internationally they call a "twenty-four-hour clock." This means they run time from 0:00 (midnight and the start of the day) to 24:00 (midnight and the end of the day). So 15:30 (pronounced fifteen thirty) is 3:30 p.m. "US" time, which is actually 12:00 p.m. plus three and a half hours, which gives you 15:30. It is actually easier to use a twenty-four-hour clock, which avoids any confusion that comes from a.m. versus p.m., especially for train and bus schedules, but many Americans are not used to this.

Dates can be more confusing. In the US, we normally use the format month, date, year. In many countries of the world, they use date, month, year. So, think about the following examples:

---

61   The World Clock – Worldwide, accessed August 26, 2020.

American Dates		Other Countries' Dates		Confusing?
March 31, 2012	3/31/12	31 March 2012	31/3/12	No
March 8, 2012	3/8/12	8 March 2012	8/3/12	YES!!! When numbers only are used: are we indicating March 8 or August 3?

Interestingly, the US military follows "military time" and uses the date format that "other countries" use.

For measurements, most of the world uses the metric system—so you will find meters, kilos, kilometers, and so forth. Only three countries do not use the metric system: the US, Myanmar, and Liberia. And most places use Celsius instead of Fahrenheit for temperature. Having a conversion table comes in handy. You can download tables from the internet before your trip or find an app for your phone.

BURQAS AND SUCH

So, we come back to the topic of burqas, which most people have seen from pictures of women in Afghanistan since the US invaded Afghanistan in 2001. They actually come in different colors, although blue is the most common. Usually you've seen them with the woman all covered, but sometimes she will throw back the front mesh part so that her face is exposed. While we in the West think of the burqa as some horrible submission of women by men, the women I have talked to actually like to wear it—it lets them be "invisible" to the men around them and not be harassed. They feel there is safety in wearing the burqa.[62]

In different parts of the world, the clothes that Muslim women wear are called different things. For example, there is the *abaya* worn on the Arabian Peninsula, the *chador* in Iran, and the *hijab*, the veil that covers the hair and neck in many parts of the world.

In Saudi Arabia, women traditionally lived under strict guardianship laws where either their father, husband, or other male guardian governed what they could do. They also had to wear an *abaya* (a long cloak) and a head scarf when they went out. While restrictions on women are starting to ease—for example, in 2018 they were finally allowed to drive—many women still wear an *abaya* when they go out so they are not harassed.[63] Interestingly, there have always been stories about how Saudi women get on the plane in Riyadh, the capital of Saudi Arabia, wearing their *abayas*. Partway through their flight to London, they go to the restroom, remove their *abaya*, and come out looking like any other hip, young woman with makeup and everything.

I visited Kabul several times between 2004 and mid-2005. Prior to my first trip, I drilled my Afghan-American coworker about what it was like for a foreign woman in Afghanistan, from how safe it was to walk around by myself (it was safe when I first went, but not so much as time went on) to when I had to wear a head scarf to how I should interact with Afghan men. Over that time period, I would wear my scarf under certain circumstances, which also depended on my

62 Caitlin Killian, "Why Do Muslim Women Wear a Hijab?," *The Conversation* (blog), January 15, 2019.

63 Nabih Bulos, "Saudi Women, Bucking Tradition, Forgo Abaya," *Los Angeles Times*, September 22, 2019.

location. When I first got there, I had a scarf, but I only wore it at certain times—getting off the plane at the Kabul airport and when I was walking down the street. I never wore it when I was in a vehicle or at the office. When I moved to Lashkar Gah in the southern province of Helmand, I did not wear my scarf in the office, but I always wore it when outside, even when I was in a vehicle (although on an earlier trip to Lash, as we called it, I did not wear my scarf all the time). When we hosted the drug czars from both the US and Afghan governments at our field site, I consciously made the decision not to wear my scarf during our field visit, although I did have it draped on my shoulders, and wore it to and from the site. I did not return to Afghanistan again until 2017 and 2018, when I visited Mazar-i-Sharif in the north—I wore my scarf while in the vehicle, but never in the office.

The various foreign women I knew in Afghanistan all made their own decisions of when they felt they had to wear the scarf or not. Some women never wore it, although they usually had one with them. Others wore it more often. Sometimes the decision was made just by what we felt comfortable with, while other times it was the situation that dictated whether or not we wore it. In some countries like Saudi Arabia, all women must wear the *abaya* when they go out of their compound, even foreign women.

WRAP-UP

As travelers, we may find it daunting to realize that each country and religion has its own cultural practices that influence interactions between them and any foreign visitor. In order to be respectful to your hosts, it is incumbent to not only study up before you travel, but also to be aware of what is being said and the body language of your counterpart. No one expects you to have complete knowledge of another country's practices but making a sincere effort counts. Researching these cultural differences is part of the learning experience and adds to the excitement of visiting another country.

I recently had a conversation with a young high school teacher, Dana Vierra, about her experiences traveling overseas and what she imparts to her students regarding the world. She has traveled a great deal, lived in South Africa for a year, and worked with the Yazidis in a refugee camp in Greece. Currently, she teaches in a rural Vermont school where she tries to raise the international curiosity of her students through the use of virtual tours through Google Earth and other websites and also by having her students cook dishes from the places they are studying. When asked about how she addresses cultural differences, she responded, "What has helped me deal with and succeed in the international arena is the understanding that everybody comes to the table with a different experience. We all didn't grow up in the same place or in the same way. It's really given me a thirst for knowledge when I go these places; I just want to know more about the culture and the history. And I think it makes me a better American citizen because I now have this view of how others look at us and how we look at others and what they've experienced." Dana articulates what I would like novice travelers to experience—traveling opens up the world and other peoples to you, which will increase your thirst for knowledge and impact how you view the world and the US.

Next up, let's talk about assumptions we make about people we encounter.

CHAPTER 5

WHAT ABOUT THAT ZIMBABWEAN SECURITY GUARD?: FALSE ASSUMPTIONS WE MAKE

———

BARBARA'S STORY

Looking at Barbara Fillip, you see a white, American woman as she stashes her groceries in the bag on the back of her bicycle to ride to her home in Arlington, Virginia. But as soon as she starts speaking, people detect an accent, and they make certain assumptions about her. Born and raised in France, Barbara's father and grandparents, whom she spent most of her young life with, were originally from Turkey. Her extended family also spanned the globe, from Turkey, to Israel, to France, to the US. Eventually, she ended up in the US and received her PhD from the University of Pittsburgh.

"My father was in the travel business, and we traveled a lot when I was growing up, mostly to Africa...Kenya, lots of travel to Kenya, but also to Japan and other places. And

I think that's how I got a sense of the bigger world around us," she shared about how she became a citizen of the world. Her family traveled to many places, but they "were still very much the foreigners" wherever they went.

When Barbara was fifteen and her brother was seventeen, their father sent them to the US to travel around the country by Greyhound bus for two months. He clearly valued international travel and had no qualms about sending his children out on their own. While they did not seek out interactions with Americans, "people were curious about who we were and what we were doing, so they would talk to us. They were concerned about our safety; they were stunned we were traveling alone."

At one point, Barbara worked in Liberia for the United Nations Development Programme (UNDP). Describing a challenging moment, she recalls a trip upcountry, outside of the capital and into the bush (uncleared land). The hosts invited her group to dinner where they brought out huge plates of very spicy rice. She remembered that it was "extremely hot, like I was probably sweating and turning all red, but I couldn't stop eating. I still remember the fire in my mouth." She ended up eating the whole thing—she realized she was a guest in a very poor country that was in a very desperate environment. She went on to say, "No matter how much they put on your plate, you just had to eat it." At times like these, citizens of the world, such as Barbara, realize how extremely privileged they are and that so many opportunities are not available to others.

Barbara's multicultural background continues to reflect itself through her daily life. When asked how her diverse background has impacted her life, she stated, "We had a lot of cultural influences from Turkey, so I make my own *boreks* (baked filled pastries) and I'm a fan of *raki*, a Turkish pre-dinner aperitif. But since I grew up in France, we took on a lot of the rituals of traditional French families, especially eating extended meals outside in the countryside."

Interestingly, you might expect Barbara's two daughters to follow in their mother's footsteps, but they instead are "90 percent American and a little French" because they learned a bit of the French language. Whereas Barbara will get on a plane to any part of the world, her daughters don't like to travel overseas; in fact, she states, "They definitely don't have the same international background or influence as I do." We discussed that it seems to us that some of the post-9/11 generation view the world as a dangerous place, more so than their parents' and grandparents' generations.

When people detect Barbara's accent, she often gets the same reaction: they praise her writing, saying "You write really well for a foreigner." This assumption always bothers Barbara, who undertook all her university and graduate studies in the US, causing her to react strongly—"Just because I was born somewhere else and I have an accent doesn't mean that I can't write in English. In fact, I can't write in French anymore."

It just goes to show, as Albert Einstein once said, "Assumptions are made and most assumptions are wrong."[64]

The way we look, the color of our skin, and the language we speak all can separate us when traveling or even in the US. But underneath these cosmetic differences, we share a common humanity, each trying to earn a living to provide for our families. Instead of being afraid or repelled by these

---

64 "Assumptions Sayings and Quotes," *Wise Old Sayings* (blog), accessed August 28, 2020.

differences and any assumptions you make, why not reach out and get to know people and build people-to-people relations? Although you can find some bad apples anywhere, assuming the worst about someone because they are different could lead you to treat others badly based on your own misconceptions. After getting to know someone, you may find you have more commonalities than differences with the people you get to know. And you just might make a new friend.

GEOPOLITICAL ASSUMPTIONS

Some assumptions we need to be mindful of center around geopolitical assumptions. As previously mentioned, the PRC is sometimes geographically referred to as mainland China but is no longer politically referred to this way. And although Hong Kong and Macau have been returned to the PRC, the US State Department still distinguishes them as separate entities. Be careful with the Republic of China (Taiwan), also referred to as the ROC or just Taiwan, which considers itself a separate country, but the PRC considers it a renegade province. At the same time, the US both commits by law to help Taiwan to defend itself, and also recognizes the one-China policy. It's a complicated dance.

Sometimes the US government, for political reasons, may decide to do something different. For instance, the US continues to refer to Burma as Burma, even though the country changed its official name in 1989 to the Republic of the Union of Myanmar, and most countries of the world use Myanmar. But the US does not recognize the name change, as we say it was done without the consent of the people.[65]

---

65   Andrew Selth and Adam Gallagher, "What's in a Name: Burma or Myanmar?," US Institute of Peace, June 21, 2018.

Even in familiar countries, we need to keep different geographies and groups straight. Northern Ireland is part of the UK and not part of the Republic of Ireland, even though they are both on the same geographic island. Additionally, the UK includes Great Britain and Northern Ireland, while Great Britain includes England, Scotland, and Wales, from which the Scots would like to break away.

Another example that I only learned about recently is that we tend to think of Finland as part of Scandinavia, but Scandinavia is actually comprised of Norway, Sweden, and Denmark. Meanwhile, the Nordic countries include Scandinavia plus Finland, Iceland, and their associated territories (Greenland, the Faroe Islands, and the Åland Islands). This distinction may seem small to us, but how do "Americans" feel about our groupings?

Previously, the US belonged to the North American Free Trade Agreement (NAFTA), which did not include Central America, even though it is geographically part of North America. Meanwhile, South Americans take issue with the US calling itself "America" and its people "Americans," as if the term refers only to the US, while they consider themselves and anyone else living in the Western Hemisphere as "Americans."[66] I have met Canadians who also lodge this complaint against us. I apologize to the citizens of other countries in the Western Hemisphere—I refer to citizens of the US as "Americans" in this book as it is not yet common to use the term "United Statesians."

If you are traveling to a sensitive area, like Northern Ireland or the PRC, it is best to try and read up on the different

---

66   Karina Martinez-Carter, "What Does 'American' Actually Mean?" *The Atlantic*, June 19, 2013.

sides of the issues. You probably will not want to raise any issues regarding sensitive topics, but you will want to be familiar enough with it so that you don't inadvertently offend someone.

ETHNIC ASSUMPTIONS

In addition to geopolitical assumptions one should be aware of, there can also be ethnic assumptions. We sometimes make assumptions based on what we think we know that may be completely wrong. An example: I was walking down the street with my father, an old Chinese man, and someone asked me whether or not he understands English. In reality, he was born and raised in California, and while he learned Cantonese first at home, he is fluent in English and graduated from college.

Another example is Alex Iseri. When you look at him, you may see a mixed-race young man with a different sounding last name—you could make certain assumptions about him. Then you find out he is from northern Michigan…you add to your assumptions about him. But as you talk with him further, you find out that until he returned to the US for college, he had spent most of his life growing up in India and Indonesia, experiencing things his American counterparts could only read about in books. Alex is known as a "third culture kid" (TCK), one that grows up in a country different than his parents.[67] When he returned to the US, Alex found he was quite different from his peers. He didn't have ties to a single location, his friends typically moved every two to five years, and he grew up outside of mainstream American

---

67 *Merriam-Webster Online,* s.v. "What Is a 'Third-Culture Kid'?," accessed August 28, 2020.

culture. Moreover, he reflects, "I'm a lot more tolerant of adversity than a lot of people in my age cohort; I have an innate ability to manage and deal with challenges." But you would never guess this by looking at him.

A further example is when I talk about colleagues I knew in Afghanistan who worked for a security company and I mention that they were Zimbabwean. People assume I am talking about Black men. In fact, they were white Zimbabweans, born and raised in Zimbabwe but subsequently kicked off their farms by the Zimbabwean government because they were white. Moreover, in addition to knowing how to protect us, they were also experts in agriculture.

In many countries, including the US, different types of people may live within a country. In Afghanistan, the main ethnic groups are Pashtun, Hazara, Tajik, and Uzbek. Pashtuns are Sunni Muslims and Pashtu speaking, while Hazaras are Shi'a Muslims and Dari speaking.[68] Without studying about Afghanistan, one might assume that the Afghans are a homogeneous group of people. And in a place like Afghanistan, misidentifying someone can actually get you killed.

Another example is the PRC, which includes twenty-two provinces, five autonomous regions, and four municipalities. China's main ethnic group is referred to as the Han Chinese, but there are also fifty-five non-Han minority groups.[69] These ethnic groups, including the Han, have differences in customs and dialects.

Many countries now include people from other parts of the world. This can be confusing for some. For example, as a Chinese-American, when I first traveled to China in the

68 *World Directory of Minorities and Indigenous Peoples*, s.v. "Afghanistan," accessed August 28, 2020.

69 The China Guide, "Chinese Ethnic Groups," updated May 23, 2019.

early 1980s, everyone thought I was Chinese. I told them that I was actually an "overseas Chinese," so then they would first ask me when I moved to the US. I responded that I was born in the US, and they would say that I didn't look like an American (because I didn't have blonde hair). Even in the US, it can be confusing. Originally, a Chinese-American meant that you were born in the US but were of Chinese ethnicity. With a new influx of Chinese immigrants since 1965 to the present, there are significant numbers of Chinese-Americans who were born overseas but have now become naturalized US citizens.

Likewise, Mozambique includes people of African origin, Indian origin, and "Arab" origin, most of whom are from Pakistan, as well as people who are mixed with all of these backgrounds. Or in South Africa, you have whites, Blacks, and "coloureds," which means being mixed race (often of Malagasy and Southeast Asian ancestry).[70] Some Americans are uncomfortable, or even shocked, to find the term "coloureds" being used in South Africa, which has been for the most part purged as an insult from our own English language.

As mentioned in Chapter 4, Californian Dana Vierra lived in South Africa for a year. When asked about being a white person in South Africa and her interactions with people from the Xhosa tribe, she stated, "I didn't really fit into any of those categories (Afrikaans or English), which maybe they would have typically avoided or not tried to get close to. It was really nice because, in their eyes, I wasn't seen as an

---

70 *Encyclopaedia Britannica Online,* s.v. "South Africa," accessed August 28, 2020.

oppressor." So, assumptions actually work both ways—how we view foreigners and how foreigners view us.

One last point about ethnic assumptions. While much of the discussion above has been placed in an overseas travel context, you can also find these types of issues in the US. We have always had a tradition of new immigrants coming to our shores, which continues to the present. In many parts of the country, immigrants settle in our communities and work alongside those whose families have been here for generations. By welcoming and interacting with these newcomers, you can learn about other countries and how to deal with other cultures in your own community, but also prepare you for overseas travel.

RELIGIOUS ASSUMPTIONS

Ethnic assumptions sometimes overlap with religious assumptions. When I look at religion, I look at it from a cultural and historical point of view, even though I have lived and traveled to parts of the world where religious conflict dominates the environment.

When you meet a Palestinian, do you assume he must be Muslim? Careful, because he could be Christian. It is estimated that Palestinian Christians make up approximately 20 percent of the thirteen million Palestinians, although they only constitute 1 percent of Palestinians in the West Bank and Gaza.[71] An Egyptian could be Muslim or Copt (an orthodox Christian denomination); an Indian could be Hindu, Muslim, Sikh, or Buddhist; an American could be Christian, Muslim, Jewish, or a non-believer. Unless a person

---

71   Ahmed el-Komi, "Gaza's Christians Blocked from Travel to Bethlehem," *Al-Monitor*, December 24, 2018.

wears distinctive clothing that reveals religion, you cannot necessarily tell this from outward appearance.

As I mentioned in Chapter 2, I lived in East Jerusalem for a year from 1994 to 1995 as part of a USAID-funded project working with Palestinian agricultural, rural electric, and handicraft cooperatives in the West Bank and Gaza. I moved there soon after Palestinian leader Yasser Arafat returned to Gaza in 1994 after twenty-seven years in exile, which signaled a hopeful phase in the Israeli-Palestinian conflict. What I did not realize until I started working on this project were the different types of Christians, Muslims, and Jews who lived in a very small area of the world. But when you dig deeper, you find the wide range of Jewish groups, including the Likud and Labor parties and other groups from the far right to the far left, the Palestinian Fatah and Hamas parties, and various Orthodox and other Christian groups, and you realize the complexities of the religious and political landscape.

When we drove into the West Bank with yellow license plates signifying Jerusalem, we would put a Palestinian keffiyeh on the dashboard to show we were pro-Palestinian once we crossed the check point, and when we came back to Jerusalem, we would remove the keffiyeh. You may have seen a keffiyeh before—usually it's a black or red checkered scarf that is traditionally used in the Middle East to shield you from the sun and blowing dust or sand.

At that time, there was some mixing of Palestinians and Israelis, with Palestinians that were living in East Jerusalem shopping and dining in West Jerusalem. But my coworkers would recall how when they were growing up in the 1970s, there was much more of a mixing between Palestinians and Israelis with Israelis coming to East Jerusalem to shop and interact. I returned to East Jerusalem and Palestine in 2003.

After the optimism of 1994, the situation had deteriorated, so there was very little mixing of Israelis and Palestinians. Each stayed in their own areas, and there was a much more adversarial view than I had known there to be. Television highlighted negative aspects of the relations—such as rocket fire onto Israel—and the tension at checkpoints between Palestine and Israel increased. Israel had erected a wall, continued its expansion of settlements in the West Bank, and built new roads to get to the settlements. This is a reality from which it will be very difficult to reverse.

Within Islam, the two main branches are Sunni and Shi'a, with approximately 90 percent of Muslims being Sunni.[72] Sunni and Shi'a share many fundamental beliefs and practices, but they differ in doctrine, ritual, law, theology, and religious organization. Sunnis regard themselves as the orthodox branch of Islam and adhere to practices based on what the Prophet Muhammad said, did, agreed to, or condemned. The Shi'a are guided by the wisdom of Muhammad's descendants through his son-in-law and cousin, Ali.[73]

In Afghanistan, the divide between groups is not only ethnic, but also religious, with its Sunni composing the Pashtuns, Tajiks, and Uzbeks, while the Shi'a are mainly of the Hazara ethnicity.[74]

Religious differences also play a role in dividing countries. Nigeria, with a population of over 206 million in 2020, is the most populous country in Africa.[75] Within the country, Muslims live mainly in the north, Christians mainly in the

72 "Sunnis and Shia: Islam's Ancient Schism," *BBC*, January 4, 2016.
73 Ibid.
74 *World Directory of Minorities and Indigenous Peoples*, s.v. "Afghanistan," accessed August 28, 2020.
75 "Nigeria Demographics," *Worldometer* (blog), accessed August 28, 2020.

south, and traditional religions are interspersed. Periodically in the newspaper you can read about religious fighting flaring up in Nigeria.

Myanmar is predominantly Buddhist but includes the Rohingya minority who are mostly Muslim. In 2017, Burma cracked down on the Rohingya, with many fleeing across the border into Bangladesh. We often think of Buddhists as peace loving, as represented by the Dalai Lama, but some can be vicious towards other religions as well.

In 2019, India's Hindu nationalist ruling party, the Bharatiya Janata Party (BJP), amended the country's citizenship law to allow Hindus, Sikhs, Buddhists, Jains, Parsees, and Christians who migrated to India from Afghanistan, Bangladesh, and Pakistan to file expedited citizenship claims. This law excludes Muslims. As the BJP fulfills its promise to create a nationwide National Register of Citizens, India's two hundred million Muslims may be asked to prove their citizenship, a tall order for residents whose families have lived in India for generations but who may have no property deeds or birth certificates, given high rates of illiteracy and voluntary registration of births.[76]

The bottom line about religion is it can be complex, contradictory, and fraught with misunderstandings for the unwary traveler who does not take the time to learn about the history and culture before traveling. You will find this research fascinating, and oftentimes much different from what we know in the US.

---

76 Suparna Chaudhry, "India's New Law May Leave Millions of Muslims without Citizenship," *The Washington Post*, December 13, 2019.

MIGRANT ASSUMPTIONS

Assumptions are also made about people who move to another country, which may be inaccurate. People leave their countries for a number of reasons. Some move to attend school and never return home. Others leave for economic reasons—their home country does not offer opportunities for them to earn a living and provide for their families. Oftentimes, someone from their family or village left and established a toehold in a country, and eventually, many of their relatives follow. That's how so many Cantonese ended up in the San Francisco area, and how Poles ended up in the Chicago area. Other people flee their home countries due to famine, war, or day-to-day violence, as can be seen when the news reports on Syrian refugees, boats full of migrants being stopped from reaching the European shores in the Mediterranean, or migrants trying to cross our southern border.

Some people are trafficked or tricked. This is probably how my paternal grandmother came to the US. In many countries, desperate people may sell their children or put their children in somebody else's care, thinking their children are being taken somewhere for a job, when in fact they are being trafficked. People often pay others to expedite their entry into a country, such as the "coyotes" who smuggle people across the Mexican-US border.[77] Sometimes they are abandoned along the way or are not freed after they cross the border. Instead, they are blackmailed to pay more money after they arrive. Many people die trying to reach a land of opportunity.

---

77 Damià S. Bonmatí, "A Day in the Life of a Coyote: Smuggling Migrants from Mexico to the United States," *Univision*, December 21, 2016.

Some people who immigrate can no longer practice their profession in their new country due to licensing requirements. For example, Chinese medical doctors or engineers who emigrate to the US often cannot practice here; instead, you find them serving as maids or cooks in Chinese restaurants. Can you imagine how this must affect their self-image? Yet they still move, looking for better opportunities for themselves and the next generation.

Temporary migrants are often the most hardworking. In December 2008, the International Labour Organization (ILO) estimated that 164 million were migrant workers.[78] Think of it this way—they come to a country to fill jobs that the local population does not want to do in order to support their families back home. Not only are they far from home, but they may only be able to return to see their families once a year, if they are lucky. For example, Mexicans come to California to harvest the fruits and vegetables that we eat—Americans have no desire to do this job, nor can we stand the backbreaking eight-hour shifts they endure in the hot sun. On my grandparents' ranch in California, the same migrant farm workers would return to help us harvest fruit every year. What about Filipina women who travel to places like Hong Kong to take care of other people's houses and children? They often are invisible, but as previously mentioned, they congregate in parks on Sundays, the one day they have off. Many Filipino men travel to the United Arab Emirates to work as construction workers. I have also flown on a plane from Johannesburg, South Africa, to Maputo, Mozambique,

---

78 "New ILO Figures Show 164 Million People Are Migrant Workers," International Labour Organization, December 5, 2018.

with a group of Chinese laborers who, it appeared, had never left their villages in China before.

When we read the news about refugees and migrants, we often make certain assumptions about them—that they are poor, illiterate, or dangerous. For the most part, they are not dangerous, they are fleeing for a better life for their families, they may be highly educated, and some are not poor. After arriving, they often work extremely hard and are thankful for the country that took them in. Except for Native Americans in the US, we all came from migrant populations at one time or the other. Just as our ancestors were looking for a better life, we should welcome migrants to our communities, help get them established, and build people-to-people relations with them. They enrich our society and make the US stronger.

On your travels overseas, you may also encounter immigrants or migrant workers and wonder why you aren't just seeing blonde Swiss in Switzerland. Remember that there is a story behind their journey to a different country and that they are probably supporting an extended family back home.

STEREOTYPES IN REAL TIME

Julien S. Bourrelle, an author who focuses on helping people communicate and connect across cultures, identifies a challenge for travelers. He notes, "People look at situations from their own cultural lens, which can lead to cultural misperceptions. It's not what you see, it's what you perceive. The world will benefit from diversity."[79] One thing we Americans often forget—we and English are not dominant in the world.

---

79 *TEDxTrondheim,* "Julien S. Bourrelle: How Culture Drives Behaviors," July 10, 2015, video, 12:07.

ETHNIC STEREOTYPES

Some stereotypes may be silly, but some may be serious, even deadly. I was once traveling in a car in Kabul with an African-American man when the police pulled the car over. My friend automatically assumed they stopped us because of him, as African-American men are often singled out by police in the US. But in fact, they pulled us over because of me—in Afghanistan, many, if not most, of the Chinese women from China serve as prostitutes. So, the police wondered why I was in the vehicle. Our Afghan driver had to explain. This tickled my friend and surprised me, as this was a new situation for me.

Another time I was in a vehicle with Pete Siu, who was wearing native Afghan dress. The Hazaras in Afghanistan look more like East Asians, so Pete could be mistaken for a Hazara, who are looked down upon by the majority Pashtuns. We had a minor fender bender in the heavy rush hour traffic in Kabul. The other driver started yelling at us and Pete got mad and wanted to go out and confront the other driver. I had to restrain Pete—the Afghans would either think he was Hazara and beat him up, or they would discover we were expats and want money from us. Our Afghan driver once again saved the day and dealt with the situation.

As mentioned above, people from a particular country or area may not be homogeneous. A Palestinian may be Muslim or Christian. A South African can be white, either an Afrikaner—who speak Afrikaans—or English-speaking; can be from one of the Black tribes; or be mixed race "coloured." These differentiations may confuse you as you get to know the people, but they are extremely important distinctions for those you meet, either at home or abroad.

Just as in the US, some people are kind and empathetic, but some are not, so it is the world over. When you look at an Afghan man, we often hold the stereotype that he is a chauvinist, but in fact when you get to know him, you will find he adores his daughters the way an American father does, wanting the best for them. At the same time, he may still have to conform to social norms. So, he will have his daughters wear their burqas when they go out, but he may also insist that his daughters go to school. One of the Afghan women I previously mentioned who worked on my project ended up going to medical school—she could not have done any of that without her father's approval and encouragement.

Many people from the West question why Muslim women wear a hijab or other covering. We often assume their male relatives are forcing them to wear it. As discussed in Chapter 4, many Muslim women prefer to wear a covering to protect themselves from unwanted attention by certain men.

Also, remember that just because someone can't speak English doesn't mean they are dumb. And no, if we raise our voice and speak louder in English, they will not understand us any better. Speaking slower and enunciating clearly may help, otherwise you can try writing something down as often non-native speakers can read English better than they can comprehend spoken English.

OCCUPATIONAL STEREOTYPES

In some parts of the world, traditional blue-collar workers spend their free time differently than we would expect. In Europe, they travel on their holidays, eat at nice restaurants, visit museums, and see the sights. When my parents and I stayed with some farmers in New Zealand, we found them very well read and knew more about US politics than we did.

And in China, I went to a friend's house to visit his family. He was a driver at the university, and his parents were workers. As we were talking, his father suddenly stood up and started singing Italian opera in Italian...and he had a great voice! More importantly, some people who may not be well-educated or who may be illiterate often know more about practical things like agriculture or fixing a car than we do. So, we should not dismiss those who have an important role to play, such as the drivers previously mentioned or someone who knows how to fix a tire when you have a flat in the middle of nowhere.

In some places overseas, those working in the hotel industry are treated completely differently than how they are treated in the US. In the US, many hotel staff tend to be part-time workers or college students, not a job they strive to make a career. But in other parts of the world, hospitality professionals take great pride in their work and their service is impeccable. Their pay is commensurate with that view, and they therefore are not working for tips.

Europeans, in particular, take hospitality very seriously and often get degrees in it before entering management positions. On the other end of the spectrum, you also have small restaurants in Europe that still have impeccable service, but are run by a family, sometimes only the husband and wife. We once found a small (six-table) restaurant in Paris, with the husband as the chef and the wife as the hostess and server. The food was so wonderful we went back again several years later on another trip. They didn't have any Michelin stars, but they made their food from the freshest ingredients they found that morning in the market.

In Asia, many hotels also offer excellent service, even small boutique hotels. You will receive a glass of juice when you check in or an orchid on your pillow, and the staff fawn over you during your stay. Only in Asia have I seen hand towels folded into the shape of bathrobes.

So, as we travel or encounter immigrants in our hometowns, we should heed what Nigerian writer Chimamanda Ngozi Adichie highlights—"The single story creates stereotypes, and the problem with stereotypes is not that they are untrue, but that they are incomplete. They make one story become the only story."[80] Go beyond the stereotype and get to know people and their stories.

ADAPTING TO DIFFERENT SITUATIONS

Part of becoming comfortable with international travel is to not jump to conclusions based on your assumptions and to have the ability to "read" the situation, which becomes more natural as you prepare and travel more. On the other hand, there may be situations that you never can get right (and may

---

80 *TEDGlobal 2009,* "Chimamanda Ngozi Adichie: The Danger of a Single Story," July 2009, video, 18:34.

never know about), and that is okay, you will never be able to achieve perfection. But if you are adaptable, authentic, and try your best to be friendly and empathetic, you will go a long way to build solid relationships with others

"Cultural intelligence" is the capability to relate and work effectively across cultures.[81] Some things are easy to understand—you see an old woman struggling to open a door with her hands full of groceries, you know that you should go and hold the door open for her. But other situations are less clear.

Sometimes, we just can't read a situation, but as long as you try to be respectful, that's the best you can do. Other times, we need to read the subtle hints, which may be different from what we are used to. When you hear Chinese people speak in Mandarin, it has a melodic sort of cadence. But if they speak in Cantonese, what sounds like yelling and arguing may just be a pleasant conversation, but since you don't understand Cantonese, you wouldn't know this. By putting on our cultural intelligence hats, we can look for subtleties that have us realize that we don't sense any anger, that there may even be joking, or they're just talking loudly!

When Susan and I traveled together in China, we worked out a system. When it was appropriate (i.e., to get better service), we had her deal with the situation with her white face. But other times, like to get things at a cheaper price, we would have me deal with the situation. In 1989, during the Tiananmen Square Massacre, Susan and I were traveling in China on a train from Urumqi to Beijing where we were going to connect to the Trans-Siberian Railway to end up in Finland. Due to the situation, the authorities cut train

---

81   "About Cultural Intelligence," Cultural Intelligence Center, accessed August 26, 2020.

service to Beijing, so we ended up in the central Chinese city of Zhengzhou and needed to find other means to get out of the country. We decided to try to buy plane tickets to Guangzhou, in the south and close to the Hong Kong border. Given the chaos and uncertainty around us, we would normally have Susan go and buy the tickets. Unfortunately, she had to wait for a call from the US Embassy. So, I set out to buy the tickets. When I got to the airline office, a mob of people surged towards the counter—all Chinese, so I blended right in (not a good thing). To get waited on, I pushed my way forward (that is what you need to do in China), waving our American passports. Luckily, the passports worked, and I bought the plane tickets.

An American friend who was teaching in Beijing also learned that in order to get on a bus or subway in China, you had to push your way in, using your elbows to the fullest extent possible. Initially she couldn't bring herself to do this, but then came to realize she had to participate if she was ever to get onto public transportation. She once went to Hong Kong for a few days. As she got on the subway, she started using her elbows to push people aside as she saw Chinese faces around her. She forgot she wasn't in China and they were Hong Kongers who are more polite (and queue up) than their compatriots across the border. Needless to say, they gave her dirty looks and wondered about her.

Similarly, Chinese people often have a quirky (at least as Americans see it) way of responding. They could be telling you a story about how their family suffered during a famine and suddenly they will start laughing about it. From your perspective, this is totally inappropriate and bizarre. From their perspective, they are embarrassed about it, so their reaction is to laugh. Your initial reaction will probably be to be horrified, but then you should probably just move on. Don't think of them as crazy; accept the cultural difference.

At the same time, Chinese can be very blunt about things. They will look at you and say how fat you are. This is a contradiction when they won't say other things because they don't want to lose "face." They see comments such as this one to be just very matter of fact, and they don't have a problem verbalizing them. Plus, at one point in time, being fat was a complement, as it meant you had plenty of food to eat.

In the US, we live in a multicultural world with many ethnicities living here. Sometimes you can tell them apart, other times you can't. But when a white person travels to Asia or Africa, all of a sudden, he becomes the minority, which is unsettling for a lot of people. Susan never knew what it was like to be a minority until she moved to China where suddenly she felt adrift in a sea of dark-headed people. It's sometimes disconcerting to go from one culture to another. I know I found it strange coming back to the US and seeing blonde, brunette, and red hair colorings after spending a year in China.

I feel like a chameleon sometimes. When I first learned to talk, I only spoke *Heungsaan*. But when I was three or four, my cousins only spoke English, so I began to bite them because we couldn't communicate. My parents realized they needed to teach me English, to the detriment of my *Heungsaan*. I grew up with a large extended family around me—all Cantonese—but my hometown was a small, bedroom community outside of San Francisco, with the population being at least 95 percent white. We celebrated Chinese holidays, like Chinese New Year and the day to sweep the graves, but we also celebrated Easter, Thanksgiving, and Christmas, not because we were religious, but because it is the "American" thing to do, AND we wanted to have a great meal!

But growing up, I carried the label "banana," yellow on the outside and white on the inside, since I grew up in a predominantly white town. The only time I was "Chinese" was within my family. But I still ran into prejudice growing up, getting teased for what I looked like. Even though I lived in China for two years, Chinese from China are different from us ABCs (American Born Chinese), and I am still more comfortable with non-Chinese friends rather than Chinese friends.

People like Barbara have had to adapt to the culture of where they have moved to. While she brings her Turkish and French background with her, she also has assumed American traits as well and can now write better in English than in French. There are other examples of people living in another country for so long that their native tongue gets rusty, they miss learning the latest slang, and they may have troubles expressing themselves in their original language. On the flip side, a friend from college of Mexican ethnicity had lived in the US since she was quite young. She spoke English with a Spanish accent, so you would assume that she was fluent in Spanish. While she was fluent in spoken Spanish, she could not write in Spanish as she had no clue where to put the accents on the words.

WRAP-UP

It is easy for people to look at someone and make certain assumptions, but just as we ourselves are complex human beings, so are the people with whom we are interacting. Additionally, what we sometimes look at as a black and white situation can actually be multifaceted, such as the

Palestinian-Israeli situation, which covers geopolitical, ethnic, and religious issues. And what do we think about migrant populations? Do we look at them for who they are and why they have moved, or do we make certain assumptions about them?

We need to look beyond what we see externally to get to know the person for who he is, not for who we think he should be. Instead, we need to build meaningful people-to-people relations. Different does not connote bad or scary. We can be stronger and more effective if we work together to address both global and local issues.

As Mark Twain said in *The Innocents Abroad*, "Travel is fatal to prejudice, bigotry, and narrow-mindedness, and many of our people need it sorely on these accounts. Broad, wholesome, charitable views of men and things cannot be acquired by vegetating in one little corner of the earth all one's lifetime."[82] I think citizens of the world can all subscribe to Mark Twain's view.

Next up, let's discuss changes in technology.

---

82   Goodreads, "Mark Twain > Quotes > Quotable Quote," accessed August 28, 2020.

CHAPTER 6

BOOKING AN INTERNATIONAL LONG-DISTANCE CALL: ADAPTING TO TECHNOLOGY

LIZ'S STORY

The radio crackled as the Marine guard (Cedar, his call sign) from the US Embassy hailed Liz Kauffman (02, her call sign) on an open line for everyone to hear.

> 02, 02, this is Cedar, over.
> Cedar, Cedar, this is 02, over.
> 02, your father is on the line and wants to know when you can take a call, over.
> Cedar, can you ask whether the call is urgent? over.
> Pause.
> 02, your mother has to have surgery, over.

Cedar, please ask my dad to call 326-459 in one hour, I'll come to the embassy, over.

02, roger that, over.

Thank you, Cedar, over and out.

And that is how Liz, and everyone else listening in to that radio frequency in Dar es Salaam, Tanzania, in 1987 found out her mom was having surgery. Times have certainly changed when everyone now carries around at least one mobile phone in their pocket.

Liz served at the US Embassy in Beijing with Susan. She and her family experienced the life of a diplomat and expatriate, including the accompanying technological changes, as they moved from Tanzania to China to Canada to India. As a public outreach diplomat, she focused on expanding and strengthening the relationship between the people and government of the US and those of the country where she was posted, including bridging cultural understanding. Coming from western Pennsylvania, did Liz always want to be a diplomat?

She credits her interest in international affairs to her aunt and uncle who traveled a lot overseas. "Back then they took slides and snapshots, so they always presented slideshows showing my uncle's family riding camels across the desert in Saudi Arabia or meeting up with elephants in India, and it looked fascinating." Additionally, her dad traveled to China in 1980, soon after China reopened to the West, to help them set up power generation facilities. "My dad then hosted Chinese engineers so they could learn what engineers were doing in the States." When she met some of the Chinese engineers who came from a country that had been closed off to the West for thirty years, her interest in international issues grew.

Her mother's family emigrated from Italy. When they met for family gatherings, she noted a "cadence with foreign languages. So even if you don't understand the language, you get into the rhythm of it and the drama of it; sometimes you can tell whether people are having an argument in good fun or having a real argument. And listening to languages has always been pretty interesting for me." Through my own experiences, I think that many of us who travel have an ear for the cadence of foreign languages, even if we do not know the language very well, or at all.

While in a master's program in comparative literature and oral histories at Penn State University, Liz traveled to Cameroon in 1982 to conduct field work. While there, she picked up her mail at the US Embassy in the capital, Yaoundé. At some point, she realized that joining the US foreign service would provide a way to travel overseas and get paid for it! The alternative was to get her PhD in oral literature where she would collect stories in West or Central Africa. "I would have needed to learn one or more non-written languages in order to contribute to the field in a meaningful way. It wasn't the challenge of learning linguistically complex pre-literate languages, immersed in fascinating village cultures that dissuaded me. It was the commitment that serious field researchers must make. Did I want to spend much of my career far from family and friends, with very limited means to stay in touch? I wasn't ready for that."

Since Liz started traveling overseas on a high school trip to France in 1975, she experienced technology changes in real time. In Paris, she vividly remembers using travelers' checks and looking at the French Franc currency with great interest. Later, in Cameroon in 1982, she sent her family news via aerograms, a now obsolete way of sending a letter by air mail. You wrote on pre-stamped, very lightweight, blue color paper that was folded into thirds and sealed at the sides so that it was self-contained. Additionally, to call home she had to book a call at the post office twenty-four hours in advance.

In Tanzania, the homes of the US Embassy personnel did not have phones, so they used radios to communicate, as demonstrated above. Then came telexes, faxes, the internet and email, and now smartphones. Liz remembers back then that "we could focus our attention a lot more on the work that we were doing because we weren't constantly checking our phones, checking the screen, trying to figure out what's going on all at once. Having that uninterrupted time was actually a luxury."

Liz provides the following advice to potential travelers: "If you haven't been someplace, then the only thing in your mind about that place is from your imagination or a second-hand account. Don't prejudge a place, wait until you get there and then listen and learn and try not to make judgments early on. For myself, I look for the positives in people." In addition to not judging people, Liz also believes in "being very respectful to others," a common theme I find among citizens of the world.

Not only did Liz make a career of the foreign service, her two sisters also ended up overseas, one marrying an Italian and the other a South Korean. Yet their brother remained in western Pennsylvania, another example of how some people from the same family or community can become citizens of the world, while others are content, even adamant, with staying at home.

HOW HAS TECHNOLOGY CHANGED THE WORLD?

Citizens of the world need to be adaptable, as they'll encounter a variety of levels of technology and innovation along the way. Do not assume that foreign countries are less advanced than the US. For example, Europe used credit cards with chips years before the US adopted this technology. When we traveled to Europe with credit cards using a magnetic stripe, we would hold up the grocery store line as we tried to use our credit card without a chip. Sometimes the store could accommodate us, other times we had to pull out cash. European restaurants also used a handheld credit card swiper early on, when American restaurants still have yet to adopt this technology *en masse*.

While we experience technology changes at a rapid rate, some parts of the world still must adapt to what they have at hand, sometimes employing skills that Westerners have lost along the way. As we travel, we must guard against ethnocentrism, or judging another culture and believing that the values and standards of one's own culture are superior, to color one's view of the world.[83] How has technology changed in the 20th century? In "How Fast Is Technology Growing Statistics," Darina Lynkova stated, "Technology's disruptive nature continues to transform our world."[84] And changes in technology not only impact how people do things, but they also can impact their thinking and attitudes.

This chapter delves into these topics—when I moved to China in 1982, computers, mobile phones, and the internet did not exist. Let's take a mini history course on technology,

---

83 *Vocabulary.com Dictionary*, s.v. "Ethnocentrism," accessed August 31, 2020.

84 Darina Lynkova, "How Fast Is Technology Growing Statistics," *Leftronic* (blog), updated May 2020.

focused on stories from the experiences of my fellow citizens of the world, but especially of Liz's and my experiences since the 1970s, including some of the technological challenges we have faced.

CHANGES IN HOW WE COMMUNICATE

TELEPHONES

Telephones existed in China in 1982, but only high-ranking officials had them in their homes. To call home to the US, I rode a rickety green and white, packed bus for approximately an hour from my school, Zhongshan University, to downtown Guangzhou. At the Dongfang Hotel, the nicest hotel at the time, I would go to the international telephone office and "book" my call to the US, taking into consideration the fifteen-hour time difference to California. When the call went through, the phone clerk summoned me to one of the numbered telephone compartments so that I could talk to my parents. "Normal" at that time meant only speaking to them every few months, with airmail letters sent in between these infrequent, expensive calls. On those trips into town, in addition to speaking with my parents, I would take the opportunity to eat a western meal at the Dongfang, a special treat. The closest I got to Western food at the university occurred when one of the cooks at the Foreign Experts Guesthouse where I ate would cook "pizza" for the children of the foreign teachers. As he didn't have any cheese, he would shred carrots on the pizza for the cheese. At least it was orange!

Booking calls was common, whether in China, England, Cameroon, or Tanzania. Not only did Liz need to book her calls in Cameroon, she also had to "designate how long it was going to be, and it was eight dollars per minute, a fortune at the time." And because she had limited communications with her family, weeks passed before she learned of her grandmother's passing and her mother's surgery. Similarly, Susan recalls, "When I traveled to England, I didn't have a phone with me. Phones were attached to walls." This is something hard to imagine these days. Instead, she filled aerograms with her daily experiences to send to her family and she looked forward to their return letters.

Technology changed and mobile phones began to be more widely utilized in the 1990s. They first appeared on the market as big, clunky things—I remember mobile phones in Jerusalem in the mid-1990s seemed like they were a foot long—and definitely not something that you could fit in your pocket. Then, instead of needing to "book" a call, I could take a call in my office in Cairo, on a *felucca* sailing on the Nile, or on a camel riding by the pyramids. Pete actually conducted phone interviews with potential graduate schools via "sat phone" (a satellite phone) while pacing in the garden of the guest house where we stayed in Lashkar Gah. It worked and he got in!

Now our lives are contained within our smartphones, and we are in dire trouble if we lose them. Even just a few years ago, no one could have imagined how different our lives would become, even in some of the poorest areas of the world, with the advent of smartphones. Mobile phones can be found almost everywhere now, with the network of some remote places of the world more sophisticated and accessible than ours. Today in the US, you can still encounter mobile phone "dead zones" where you cannot get a mobile phone signal, yet in 2013, we made a clear phone call using our rented mobile phone on the top of Huangshan Mountain, a 3,600-foot mountain in China's rural Anhui Province. Some rural areas of the world routinely do banking and payments through their mobile phones, a still relatively new technology for Americans.

For the global traveler, we originally needed to check several things about our mobile phone before we departed for overseas:

- Did your phone have the frequency bands to allow it to be used internationally?
- Did your plan include receiving and sending calls internationally?
- What was your data plan when overseas, including how much the per minute cost would be for calls as well as the charges for data and web access?
- Did your mobile phone provider have an agreement to operate in the country you would be visiting?

As mobile phones and plans continue to change at a rapid pace, contact your phone carrier to get these questions answered, as well as whether or not you can purchase a local SIM card overseas to have a local number. Depending on your data plan, you should be vigilant, as the overseas charges can be staggering. Or you could rent a phone, either before you depart or once you are overseas.

In remote areas where you might not have mobile phone coverage or access to a landline, or if it is dangerous place, satellite phones may be the backup system you need. They tend to be bulky, expensive to use, and don't hold a charge for very long, but sometimes it is the only accessible communication link.

You may find phone numbers a bit confusing. When dialing international numbers from the US, first dial "011," then the country code, and then the number — if there is a "0" before the number, you can drop that. For example, if the number is 020-74931232 and the number is in Italy (country code 39), you would dial 011-39-20-74931232. The "0" before the number overseas usually indicates a mobile phone. If you are dialing a mobile phone number when you are in the country, then you keep the "0" — by doing this, if you call an Italian mobile number in Italy, then you would dial "020-74931232."

When you are overseas and you want to call an international number, first dial "00," then the country code, and then the number. So, if you call back to the US (country code 1), dial 001-505-555-555.

COMPUTERS AND THE INTERNET

Changes in phone technologies have been accompanied by the advent of widespread use of computers and the internet, which have greatly impacted global travelers, especially our written communications.

Back in the day, we wrote letters. As previously mentioned, for international air mail, or *par avion*, we used aerograms. We also wrote postcards that included pretty stamps from around the world. It would be so exciting to receive an aerogram or postcard. We let our parents know that we had arrived safely by writing home, which, depending on your location, could take weeks to arrive. No instantaneous communications existed. In some ways, young travelers, in particular, had more autonomy then, as our parents assumed we were safe, even though they didn't know exactly where we were. They expected us to figure things out and "act" like an adult, as we couldn't easily call home to have our parents help us out. Nowadays, if we don't check in with our parents or loved ones, they immediately think the worst.

In the early 1990s, computers and email began to appear, but only businesses had these. I lived in Jerusalem from 1994 to 1995 and still wrote letters home to my parents, as they did not have a computer or email. I remember my boss had a CompuServe account with dial-up service, and everyone thought he was cool. In 2004, while in Afghanistan with Pete, he told me about a "secret" email service that you had to be invited to join—it was called Gmail!

We now have a much easier way to communicate with others and research information. With internet access, you can communicate with any part of the world that is connected to the internet (and has electricity). Some companies own sophisticated videoconferencing equipment that makes holding global meetings easier. But global communicators can now access different programs, many of them free, such as Skype, Zoom, or WhatsApp.

Additionally, depending on your mobile phone's data plan, you can access Google Maps, Google Translate, and other travel websites, such as Trip Advisor or Yelp, at your fingertips when you travel. This makes it much easier to research travel-related information without bringing a huge guidebook. But you still might want to have a backup paper map in case you don't have internet access, or if your phone runs out of power. It's also easier to have a local person point out how to get somewhere on a paper map, especially if you don't speak a common language. You can use Uber in some countries while other countries, like Cambodia, have their own local Uber-type system.

Many of us need (or feel we need) our laptops or tablets with us at all times. The size and weight of a laptop makes it easy to bring it with us on trips, especially to access our social media platforms and keep friends and families updated in real time. Depending on where you travel, you may need to be extremely careful to keep track of your computer and your mobile phone at all times not only to keep your devices from being stolen, but also to protect against hackers who want to steal your information. Some countries are notorious for this, such as Russia and China, including at Customs (when you enter a country), when they may say that they have to check something on your computer and take it to a back room out of your sight. Unfortunately, this is an increasing occurrence at US Customs as well, especially for certain foreigners entering the US.[85] Research your destination before you leave to see if this is a concern. Some people do not think this is possible or that it won't happen to them, while other people are quite concerned about this issue. To avoid this potentiality, you could rent a mobile phone or a laptop and have minimal information on your device, as we did for China.

If you don't carry a laptop, you can frequent internet cafés and business centers around the world. You must be careful on these computers as they are publicly used — for example, avoid entering credit card information or passwords to your online banking site, and always log out of your webpages and sessions. Another concern is plugging a flash drive into someone else's computer — you can pick up a virus and then infect your own computer. Also, beware of free Wi-Fi networks—hackers can set up Wi-Fi systems that look legitimate, such as a Wi-Fi system at an airport, to steal your information. I am not a computer expert, so check with someone

---

85   Andy Greenberg, "A Guide to Getting past Customs with Your Digital Privacy Intact," *Wired*, February 12, 2017.

who understands computer security before traveling, whether domestically or overseas. Don't assume it will be okay.

While many parts of the world have internet now, you can still run into some challenges. Some places don't have mobile phone coverage or internet access. In other places, electricity is not reliable, which also affects internet service providers. There could be power outages at certain times of the day, or it could be the rainy season. I could not access the internet in my hotel in Niamey, Niger, even though it supposedly had Wi-Fi. I had to wait to get to the office to check emails; not very convenient when people in Washington, DC, five hours behind Niamey, waited for my responses.

Interestingly, computer keyboards in other countries may differ from American ones. In places like Germany, the difference will be slight (for example, being able to type an "ü"), but China and Russia will have completely different keyboards. This may be a challenge for you at internet cafés.

I try to take as many precautions as possible when I travel. As mentioned, the last time I traveled to China, I rented a mobile phone and did not bring any of my own devices. When I travel for work with my laptop and mobile phone, I never use a free Wi-Fi system at airports, and at hotels I limit my time online if their system is not password protected. My computer is password-protected, and I always lock up my computer when I am not in my room. My phone is always with me. If I have to use a flash drive, I make sure to scan it for any viruses when I get it back.

Remember to bring your power cords and plug adaptors when you travel overseas. Most, if not all, laptop and mobile phone chargers are dual voltage, so you will just need to bring the plug adaptor. But check your cord to make sure—somewhere on the cord it will say "input 100-240v" if it is dual voltage. Electrical plugs differ around the world and you must research what plug is used where you are traveling to—sometimes a country will use more than one type of plug. Make sure you bring several plug adaptors, especially if you use a mobile phone, laptop, and other device that all need charging at the same time. You can buy one device that contains several different plugs, which is convenient, but also a bit bulky. I tend to carry both the one device with several different plugs plus a few specific plug adaptors. Recently, I also started bringing a dual voltage power strip that includes USB ports, as some hotel rooms have a limited number of electrical outlets. Don't forget, when transiting through another country, you may need a different plug there, although now more places have USB ports, including some long-distance airplanes. If your plug needs a ground, that will come into play when you purchase a plug adaptor.

CHANGES IN HOW WE TRAVEL

Changes in technology have also impacted transportation modes. In the US, we take transportation for granted, but in many parts of the world it is quite different. You may find rutted, dirt roads serving as main roads, even in some capital cities; other roads that wash out during the rainy season; and some places requiring ferries to cross a river. This means that you must devote much more time to getting around, requiring a lot of patience and perseverance.

In Dar es Salaam, when Liz's housekeeper's wife wanted to see her family in her small village in the far corner of Tanzania, she endured the following ordeal. Anna would pack up her two kids and a niece who lived with her, plus gifts from the big city to take back to her family. Her younger sister traveled in to help Anna make the trip. First, they took the train, which got them to within a hundred miles of home. That took about five hours. From the train, they took a bus to reach a smaller town closer to their village. Once they unloaded everything from the bus, they chartered a boat to get them upriver. They got off the boat and walked the last three miles home through forest and meadows. Needless to say, they arrived tired, dusty, and glad to be home.

Buses in many developing countries aren't like buses in the US that give you your own seat, air conditioning, and maybe even a movie playing on long-distance trips. In many places, people cram into the rickety buses, sometimes with people sitting on the roof too. You can also find chickens and other livestock sharing your ride as they look at you from the aisles.

Liz once took a van from Yaoundé, the capital of Cameroon, to Bamenda, in the English-speaking northwest. In the US, this van would carry twelve people. But instead, they fitted the van with three parallel benches that ran from the front to the back of the passenger compartment. The van left only when the driver was satisfied with the passenger and cargo load. They lashed bales of cotton, trunks full of merchandise, banana branches loaded with fruit, dried fish, beans, and sometimes a small, live goat to the top of the van. Inside, passengers sat on the benches facing each other and interwove their thighs, so, you had two knees belonging to passengers across from you on either side of your knees. Only the back of the passenger compartment had a door.

The driver pulled out with the back door still open and a couple of people holding on to the back of the van. As they jumped up onto the bumper, the driver slammed on the brakes and all the passengers jolted forward from their stupor, making room for the last two, who wedged their hips in and closed the door before anybody exhaled. The van held twenty-one passengers, with no air conditioning, the sun beating down, and dry season red soil particles suspended in the air. But everyone agreed to leave the windows open, so passengers were coated with reddish, powdery soil that reached into their throats and lungs. While they didn't know each other at the outset, six hours later they'd learned each other's jokes, songs, and children's names. It was best not to look out the windows at the condition of the roads as they wound up into the hills. More modern, paved roads now exist, but that only means drivers drive faster, not necessarily more carefully.

Transport in China has changed dramatically over the years. In the 1980s, you rode trains to travel long distances. They had different categories of service—sleeper class, soft seat, hard berth, and hard seat. The sleeper class contained four berths and doilies on the tables and the conductor brought you tea. In hard berth, it was like a free-for-all, with four berths stacked on top of each over in a space meant just for two berths. People jammed into hard berth and hard seat, including passengers standing in the aisles when they weren't able to purchase a seat. Some people stood for hours. I've ridden trains in China for what seemed like days, with the longest from Urumqi, in China's far northwest, to Beijing, which takes approximately forty hours. If you ride the regular train from Beijing to Shanghai, it takes at least fifteen hours, while you now arrive in four hours and eighteen minutes on the new bullet train. And the interiors of Chinese trains now resemble the inside of an airplane. Planes are also a popular way to travel now.

China needs these vast transport modes to accommodate the "world's biggest human migration"—this year estimated to be three billion trips—occurring in China during the Chinese New Year celebration.[86] Many Chinese have left their villages for economic opportunities in the cities, but return home to celebrate New Year's, which is sometimes their only trip home during the year.

Beijing's subway system opened on October 1, 1969, which also happened to be their National Day to commemorate the establishment of the PRC in 1949.[87] The second largest city in China behind Shanghai, Beijing has an estimated population of 19.4 million in 2020.[88] In 1989, I stayed with an American friend who was teaching in Beijing at a school on the outskirts of town at the time, and at the end of a subway line. To get on or off the subway in Beijing required planning. One time, I was trying to figure out how to get off the train amid the crush of people around me, when suddenly, to my horror, I was lifted off my feet by the people around me, leaving me hovering several inches above the floor in suspended animation. At last the crowd moved towards the door, and I found my feet back on the floor, able to quickly move out of the train.

In 1980, basically no private citizens owned cars, which were only for officials and had curtains covering the back window.[89] Even into the mid-1980s, cars were scarce and the only people who knew how to drive had learned in the military. When I studied in Guangzhou from 1982 to 1984, my

86 Maggie Hiufu Wong, "3 Billion Journeys: World's Biggest Human Migration Begins in China," *CNN*, January 10, 2020.

87 Railway Technology, "Beijing's Metro, Beijing Subway Development," accessed August 31, 2020.

88 Nick Routley, "Meet China's 113 Cities with More Than One Million People," *Visual Capitalist*, February 6, 2020.

89 Jamie Fullerton, "The Collector Using Classic Cars to Share the History of Communist China," *CNN*, updated January 18, 2017.

parents visited twice, and we hired a car and driver to travel back to their villages in the Pearl River Delta. To get to my father's village in Taishan, we had to cross a number of rivers, and no bridges existed. Instead, you had to wait for ferries, which meant it took a long time to go less than one hundred miles. But there was a silver lining. The people waiting for the ferry were a captive audience, so various food hawkers plied their wares. I discovered the freshest, most wonderful buns while waiting for a ferry! Now bridges cross the rivers, cutting down on the travel time, but that also means no fresh buns.

The number of private cars in China increased dramatically following the severe acute respiratory syndrome (SARS) outbreak from 2002 to 2004.[90] People were afraid to use public transportation, and their income had reached a point where they could purchase their own automobiles with the assistance of newly available car loans.[91] At the same time, expatriates living in Beijing noted that the concept of repaying a loan was not yet understood, so Chinese consumers all bought cars not realizing they had to pay the money back. This surge in private cars led to the decline of the bicycle, which had become ubiquitous with the advent of the PRC. Today, few people in China use bicycles for transportation and over two hundred million private cars on the road in China, leading to massive traffic jams.[92]

90 "SARS Spurs China Car Buying, but Tough Road Ahead," *Automotive News* (blog), May 14, 2003.

91 Joe Studwell, *The China Dream: The Quest for the Last Great Untapped Market on Earth* (New York: Grove Press, 2005), 493.

92 "China Has over 200 Million Private Cars," *Xinhuanet,* January 7, 2020.

INGENUITY WHEN TECHNOLOGY IS NOT AVAILABLE

Despite the advances in technology, sometimes it becomes irrelevant when technology is not available, and as a result, quick-thinking and creativity regain value. As you travel, you may encounter situations where innovation and ingenuity reign, as Liz relates in a couple of stories.

As the movie theater had not survived the years-long recession in Dar es Salaam, Tanzania, in her role as a public outreach diplomat at the US Embassy in the mid-1980s, Liz decided to host a film screening on the lawn at her house. While her staff set up, they dug a trench to bury the extension cord so guests wouldn't trip. As they did so, a shovel sliced into a water pipe, shooting water six feet into the air and submerging half the yard with two inches of water. They thought about canceling the event, but that would be difficult as few people had phones back then and they didn't have enough staff to travel the rutted dirt roads to notify everyone. As they looked around in despair, their cook (who doubled as their household manager) told them not to worry. He left the compound and came back with ten large buckets and twenty neighbors, including children, carrying cups and ladles, with the smallest children carrying spoons. More neighbors arrived and they scooped out as much water as possible, then used blankets, bedspreads, and towels to soak up more water so that the guests wouldn't sink into the mud. Crisis averted and Liz paid the neighbors for their assistance as well as invited them to stay to watch the film.

Even paper maps could not always help drivers find their destinations in the Tanzanian countryside back then. You had to stop and ask for directions. They could easily relay simple directions, like turn left at the next intersection and drive for thirty minutes. But otherwise, the person you asked might feel obligated to take you there personally. Once Liz's family asked a lone Masai herder walking along the highway for directions. His pierced ears each sported decorative travel shampoo bottles that were three-fourths of an inch in diameter. First he placed his wooden staff, taller than he, in the back of the car and then gathered his scotch plaid robe onto his lap. He took them to their destination, and then they took him back to his destination. He spoke some English and shared stories about the cattle he herded, as had his ancestors.

CHANGES IN ATTITUDE – WHAT HAPPENED IN CHINA

I have observed that changes in technology led to changes in the attitudes of the people. A good example is China. Since my first trip to China in 1980, China's startling societal changes over the past forty years resulted directly from the role that technology advances played. After a civil war, the Chinese Communist Party established the PRC in 1949. Soon after, they closed themselves off from the West and did not reopen their doors until 1979. As previously discussed, curious to know what China was like, my parents and I joined a Pan Am tour of China in August 1980.

After we crossed the border from Hong Kong, we got on a Chinese train and headed for Guangzhou, the former Canton. My "old home"—which is how the Chinese refer to the area of your ancestral home—is in Guangdong Province, with Guangzhou as its capital. As soon as the train pulled out, we noticed a marked difference—on the Hong Kong side, there was hustle and bustle and neon lights all the way up to the border. On the Chinese side, all of a sudden, we were transported back to 1922, seeing a China exactly how my grandmother described. There were no lights, only rice paddies with men walking behind water buffalo plowing the fields. Peasants in conical hats had poles across their right shoulders, each walking in a swaying motion to balance the baskets on either end of the pole. From the train, we occasionally passed villages off in the distance that were made of mud, some with tiled roofs.

All of China seemed stuck in a previous era. Everything seemed drab—the people wore drab green or blue "Mao suits" with cloth shoes and referred to each other in the Communist manner, as "comrade."[93] Very few cars were on the road, which were packed with bicycles. There was no air conditioning, very few high-rise buildings, and not even access to very many books. We witnessed a near riot when a bookstore opened with a new supply of books and people, who had been queued up, pushed and shoved their way into the store. They seemed desperate to buy books to sate their thirst for knowledge. As we drove from the airport into Beijing, we noticed groups of people sitting on the ground. It took us a while to understand that they were reading and playing

93   Lauren Mack, "What Is a Mao Suit?" *ThoughtCo.* (blog). July 3, 2019.

cards under the light from the streetlamps, a phenomenon I have also seen in Africa.

In 1982, I returned to Guangzhou to start a year abroad program through UCLA at Zhongshan (Sun Yatsen) University; I ended up staying for two years. There were four foreign exchange students (two of us from the US and two from Australia) and a handful of foreign teachers. Many of the Chinese who supported the Foreign Experts' Guesthouse, where the foreign teachers lived and where we ate, had recently returned to Guangzhou from the countryside where young people had been "sent down" for re-education during the decade-long Cultural Revolution, which had officially ended six years prior.[94]

Many people no longer wore the drab Mao suits and they seemed livelier. There were a few more vehicles on the roads, primarily taxis, and still a lot of bikes. Rationing continued on such items as good bicycles, rice, and pork. Being in the military or a Communist Party member were avenues to success and special treatment. Foreigners shopped at the Friendship Stores, which were, along with the hotels for westerners, off limits to Chinese. When you wanted to buy something in a department store, you went to the counter and once you got the clerk's attention, which could take a while as they often ignored the customers, you asked for the item. As the clerk wrapped up your item, you went to the cashier station to pay for it. You would then bring your receipt back to the clerk, who would then give you your item.

When my parents visited at Christmas, they walked into my room and my dad said, "You know, I've lived in some

---

94 Tom Phillips, "The Cultural Revolution: All You Need to Know about China's Political Convulsion," *The Guardian*, May 10, 2016.

pretty bad places, but this place…!" I lived in a graduate dorm with one Chinese roommate, and we slept on a wood plank with a mosquito net. When you walked into my room, there was a doorway to the right into the bathroom. A cement slab served as the sink and a wall partitioned off the toilet, a porcelain hole in the cement floor. We had running water, but only cold water. To get hot water, we had to heat the water in a bucket on a hot plate and bathe in the cement area next to the porcelain hole.

We could also get our thermoses filled with hot water from the hot water station, which was prevalent throughout China at the time. I also used the hot plate to boil noodles for breakfast. In the hot, semi-tropical summers, we only had a fan to cool us. Ants were a problem, too; I once hung a bag with food in it from the wire we used to hang the mosquito nets for the bed and our wet towels—the ants found it by marching across the wire to the bag, and then marching down the bag to the food. I finally learned that to protect my food, I needed to get an enamel dish of water, put the food in another dish, and put it in the dish of water, forming a moat around the food. It turns out ants can't swim, so my food was then safe!

Compared to American dorm rooms, people would consider my dorm room sparse and barren, but there it was luxurious. Chinese undergraduate students lived in a room with eight people and the communal bathroom down the hall, laundry was hanging everywhere. On one of our first days in China, the other American student, who lived next door, ran screaming out of her room. When I went next door, I found her Chinese roommate trying to "shoo" a huge spider out of the clothes cupboard. It took some getting used to, but eventually my dorm became "home."

During the time I lived in Guangzhou, more food became available and the Chinese slowly started buying refrigerators for their homes. Previously, they kept their fresh meat and any leftovers in a screened cabinet (unrefrigerated) until they were ready to use it.

As I mentioned in Chapter 3, south of the Yangtze River—which divides China into north and south—there is traditionally no indoor heating. You might think, well Guangzhou is subtropical, it's south of the Tropic of Cancer, and never falls below freezing, so what's the problem with no heat? But Guangzhou has a humid, penetrating cold in the winter, aggravated by the fact that you never can get warm (no heat) and they don't drink hot soup in the winter. To cope, we wore multiple layers of clothes, made of cotton or polyester; no, they didn't wear wool or gloves. In fact, every winter, many Cantonese get frostbite on their toes, which they call "little radishes," due to the cold, dampness, lack of heat, and thin socks they wear. The Chinese built the buildings, whether dorms, apartments, or classrooms, out of uninsulated concrete—cold and damp. When Susan and I visited Guangzhou in the winter of 1989, Susan, whose heritage is Finnish and her hometown is on the Canadian border, froze in the damp cold and tried to warm up under a heavy, cotton quilt while fully dressed. She almost fell over when my Chinese friend came to visit and complained how stuffy the room was, so she threw open the windows to air it out and let in the cold, fresh air.

Fast forward to China in 2008 and 2012. The year 2008 is significant as Beijing hosted the XXIX Olympiad. To prepare for this world event, the Chinese focused on improving the transportation infrastructure and building venues to host the Olympics. As I tuned in to the games from the US, I saw that China had changed drastically since my first visit in 1980. Taking advantage of technological advances, and often able to leapfrog over technologies that were almost already obsolete, China transformed itself into a modern, powerful, and rich (at least in many areas of China) country in a little over twenty-five years. The Olympics served as China's "coming out party" and they wanted to demonstrate they were a world power.[95] I sat awestruck as I watched the opening ceremony, especially as I thought back to when I first crossed the border into China.

In 2012, I traveled to China for the first time since 2003. I found not only a different place from the previous time I visited, but the changes in the attitudes and dress of the Chinese people struck me the most. I would never have imagined that the Chinese people could change so much— their young people sounded, looked, and acted like young people anywhere. And everyone seemed to have a mobile phone. I saw Lamborghinis and Porsches driving down the streets of Nanjing; I could shop in Tiffany's and Cartier in

95   Lee M. Sands, "The 2008 Olympics' Impact on China," *China Business Review*, July 1, 2008.

the bigger cities; I ate at bustling restaurants; and I found very few bicycles on the streets. In less than thirty-two years, China transformed itself from a backward, sleepy country to a dynamic, modern economy. After remaining stuck in a peasant society for centuries prior to 1980, China virtually changed itself overnight.

WRAP-UP

Without advances in technology, we could not visit the places we can now, nor even easily learn about different places from the comfort of our own living room. We find that technological changes affect many people in the world today, but some corners of the world still have not seen technology reach their villages. Yet you also might be surprised that while a dirt road may take you into the bush, once you get there you find a repurposed shipping container serving as the local mobile phone dealer with people paying their bills via their mobile phones.

At the same time, we never know what's on the horizon. As we ended 2019, global travel had become a "normal" thing for many people, whether for work, pleasure, or to escape war. But then, almost out of nowhere, the Novel Coronavirus Global Pandemic hit, and within weeks, international travel virtually ground to a halt. As we adapt to "shelter in place" modalities, technology assists us to continue working or studying from home, whether we utilize remote conferencing, webinars, or online learning. Once the pandemic passes, it is hard to believe we can go back to our previous "normal," but we currently cannot yet fathom what our "new normal" will be like. Still, global travel will resume at some point, utilizing technology to advance societies and further our exploration of the world.

As we face the unknown, we can adhere to Leon C. Megginson, Professor of Management and Marketing at Louisiana State University at Baton Rouge's paraphrase of Charles Darwin: "According to Darwin's Origin of Species, it is not the most intellectual of the species that survives; it is not the strongest that survives; but the species that survives is the one that is able best to adapt and adjust to the changing environment in which it finds itself."[96]

Next up, let's discuss how to prepare for adversities.

---

96   University of Cambridge, Darwin Correspondence Project, "The Evolution of a Misquotation," accessed August 31, 2020.

CHAPTER 7

THERE IS NO NEED FOR PANIC[97]: WHAT TO DO IN THE FACE OF ADVERSITY

BRIAN'S STORY

As a child, Brian Taussig-Lux first became interested in reaching out across the globe through his shortwave radio. "I still can't tell you whether it was the technical side of it or the reaching out to another place that got me interested. But I became fascinated by what was going on around the world and listening to stations that provided a very different perspective on what was happening." From that beginning, and after a temporary detour to electrical engineering, Brian now heads Untours, a travel company that his uncle and aunt, Hal and Norma Taussig, founded in 1975.

I may be biased, as Susan and I have been on eight Untours trips and my parents were Untourists before us. We fully subscribe to the experience Untours offers; living like

---

97 The Nigerian pilot announced as the plane filled with smoke.

a local by staying in one place for a longer period of time provides a much different experience than getting on and off tour buses with a group. It is a fantastic way to travel to Europe. We would not have found the previously mentioned homemade chips and fresh prawns at that park in southern Spain without being on an Untours trip.

Brian touts Untours' purpose, noting, "We want to foster a healthy and healing society that unites people of different cultures and economic statuses." When asked why he travels, Brian replied, "To meet and have conversations with different people and to see things and experience things."

Brian experienced overseas travel for the first time when he spent a summer in Switzerland as a teenager helping Uncle Hal prepare for the arrival of Untours guests. "Throughout my life I constantly experience challenges and most of them have been overseas," Brian commented. This leads him to always plan and prepare yet also be flexible and improvise when faced with adverse situations. Once in Bolivia during the rainy season, he recalled, "We needed to take a train from Potosi to Sucre. They don't have train schedules there, so you just go to the train station and check the chalkboard that tells you when the train is going to come that day, they don't even give you a day's notice." The train left the station and was going over a mountain when it screeched to a halt. Brian continued, "The conductor came through and said that the train had derailed so they would take the passengers back to Potosi."

Brian thought this was "the craziest, most absurd thing in the world." Why would the passengers want to return to Potosi when they just got on the train there to go to Sucre? So, he went to each person to take his own survey to see if passengers wanted to go back to Potosi or continue to Sucre.

In the end, he convinced the conductor to arrange for the passengers to proceed to Sucre. Without his quick thinking, he would have ended up back in Potosi. As travelers, we often must think on our feet to deal with a situation, sometimes in the couple of minutes before a train pulls out of a station!

These days there are plenty of ways for people to travel, yet Untours serves a purpose. The staff of Untours arrange the logistics for vacations to Europe for a one to two week stay in one location, allowing you to really get to know the place. For example, they vet agritourism apartments in Tuscany, arrange rental cars, and greet you at the Florence airport. They offer a welcome briefing, then you are on your own to do what you like during your stay, with optional classes available. Halfway through your stay, they organize a dinner so that the Untourists can get together, have a great meal, and share notes on where they have visited.

When asked what is unique about Untours, Brian continues, "We provide people with an extra level of assurance and support, which is valuable to them. We also expose them to the kinds of experiences that are not going to happen if you're on a regimented tour, or even if you're traveling independently." Brian adds that "travelers also need room for spontaneity and serendipity, and I think we offer that." As part of the pre-departure package, Untours provides materials and resources so that their clients can prepare and study up before they go. I know that we loved receiving the pre-departure packet from Untours, signaling we had an upcoming trip and would visit many of their suggested sites and local festivals.

Brian's advice for travelers is to "not assume you know everything and that everybody's like you. Keep your eyes open, try to learn what to do, and try to understand what's going on, but also realize there are plenty of situations where there's no way you will know what's going on." He also raises a point that many of us citizens of the world subscribe to: just try to do your best and most people will give you lots of credit for trying.

Brian wholeheartedly supports the view that traveling and learning about new places builds relationships and understanding across the globe, but it can also be challenging. Prepare for the places you will travel to, but also realize challenges may, and probably will, arise. Being attentive, creative, and flexible will help mitigate the unexpected circumstance, if not address it completely, as Brian learned in Bolivia.

WHAT CAN GO WRONG?

Whenever you travel, there are opportunities for things to go wrong. It could be as small as getting lost, waking up late due to jet lag, or not being able to sleep at all due to jet lag. Maybe you are having problems dealing with and understanding the people around you. Or you could face a natural or man-made disaster.

With the internet available in many places these days, you may be able to research information in real time on how to do deal with issues you encounter. Sometimes you will go for years without any problem, or encounter one problem on a trip, or maybe one trip will throw a bunch of problems at you. Prepare for adversity; maybe it won't happen, but then you are still ready for whatever comes your way. It's just like carrying an umbrella; when you have one it might never rain, but if it does rain you are confidently prepared.

Sometimes when we face adversities overseas, we blame them on different peoples and cultures rather than realize that we can also encounter them in the US. The difference is just that we feel they are "normal" here, so we take them in stride. Apply this perspective to your overseas travel and you will feel more comfortable facing challenges you meet. And remember British essayist Pico Iyer's words of wisdom: "It's not our experiences that form us but the ways in which we respond to them."[98] I keep these words in mind, especially when I see others experiencing meltdowns as I travel. Things may be happening, but often all I can do is remain calm and patient.

And while you may be apprehensive about traveling, think of my friend Laura Gerdsen Widman. After parachuting into Borneo, Indonesia, through the American Field Service exchange program when she was in high school, she noted, "I was apprehensive before I left, but once I got there, the experience was just so stimulating, everything was so beautiful, it was a feast for the senses." You can choose to focus on the negative, or you can see the beauty around you—it's your choice.

DELAYS AND OTHER LOGISTICAL ISSUES

Some delays you encounter may be completely out of your control. In 2010, the Eyjafjallajökull volcano erupted in Iceland and disrupted air traffic in Western and Northern Europe for six days due to the volcanic ash that drifted from Iceland to Europe.[99] Not only did it disrupt travel within Europe, but it also cut links from North America to Africa, the Middle East, and even some parts of Asia that transit through Europe. You may have been trying to get back to the US from Kenya, but you could have been stuck

---

98 Goodreads, "Pico Iyer > Quotes," accessed September 3, 2020.
99 Bente Lilja Bye, "Volcanic Eruptions: Science and Risk Management," *Science 2.0*, May 27, 2011.

in Kenya, or you could have been halfway home and gotten stuck in Amsterdam. Even after the ash cleared, it took days to reschedule everyone and clear the backlog of people. Although this was a significant event, it was nowhere near as impactful as the eruption of the Laki volcanic fissure in southern Iceland from June 1783 to February 1784, which caused climate changes that created food scarcity, a major factor leading to the French Revolution in 1789.[100]

More recently, by March 2020, the COVID-19 epidemic ballooned into the Novel Coronavirus Global Pandemic, affecting travelers throughout the world. Countries reacted differently, with some cutting off travel from specific countries while most required travelers to go into self- or forced quarantines for fourteen days. Many travelers got stuck when the airlines canceled their flights, or the country they were visiting closed its borders.[101]

While travelers can't anticipate events like these, it is still better to prepare for potential disruptions than to feel lost at sea. Whenever I travel, I always make sure I'm prepared in case something happens, and if you travel a lot, it will happen at some point. In my carry-on luggage, I bring what I might need if I have to unexpectedly spend the night somewhere, including an extra pair of underwear, a toothbrush and toothpaste, a phone charger, and plug adapters, for example. I also now carry a power strip with USB ports—this can come in handy if there are flight delays and limited electrical outlets in an airport. You will make new friends as people realize

---

100 Greg Neale, "How an Icelandic Volcano Helped Spark the French Revolution," *The Guardian*, April 15, 2010.

101 United Nations World Tourism Organization (UNWTO), "Impact Assessment of the COVID-19 Outbreak on International Tourism," updated May 2020.

that you can help them charge their devices. Additionally, I carry some US dollars (including some small bills), at least two credit cards, and two ATM cards. Make sure you include your medications and an extra pair of eyeglasses. Some people also carry a change of clothing. As events unfold, check with your airline, the US State Department, or news agencies for updates, as appropriate.

Weather can also delay travel. If you were traveling from Colorado to France via Washington, DC when "snowmegeddon" hit in 2010, you would have been surprised by two to three feet of snow paralyzing the Washington, DC area for two days, and closing airports along the East Coast from the Mid-Atlantic states northward.[102] Depending on when you are traveling, you may want to route your flights through certain airports to reduce travel delays due to potential bad weather.

People have preferences for airports to transit through for their trips. For my first trip to Albania, I decided to transit through Rome's Leonardo da Vinci Airport. It sounded so cool to go through Rome and, of course, I love Italian food! In the end, it turned out this was not such a good idea. The airport had stylistic chairs to sit in, but they were made of metal mesh and not comfortable to sit in for long periods of time. And we did sit for a long time as our flight was delayed— it turned out strikes and other flight delays are commonplace in Rome. Later I learned it was much better to fly to Albania via Vienna, Austria, where everything is on time (usually)! My least favorite major airport, though, is Paris' Charles de

---

102 Climate Signals beta, "Snowmageddon February 2010," updated December 4, 2018.

Gaulle—I always seem to have some type of problem there and the food is not very good, even though you are in France.

Some people like to fly via Munich instead of Frankfurt because Munich is a smaller, less busy airport compared to Frankfurt. If you are transiting through London, check which airport your flight arrives at and from which airport your next flight departs. While London Heathrow is the main airport, depending on your destination, some flights only go through Gatwick airport. That means if you arrive at Heathrow, you then must add time to either take a taxi (very expensive) or a bus to Gatwick. Even in Washington, DC, you need to be sure which airport you are flying into (we have three: Dulles, west of Washington; National in Arlington, Virginia, near downtown Washington; or BWI, near Baltimore) and which one you are flying out of, in case it is different. Additionally, if you are trying to fly to Washington Dulles (airport code IAD—every airport has a three-letter identifying code), make sure you purchase your ticket for Dulles, as I have known some people who had mistakenly purchased a ticket for Dallas, Texas (airport code DFW).

Then there is the luggage issue. Some travelers will do carry-on luggage only, while others check luggage. Some of this is personal preference, but it may be dictated by where you are flying and whether you are in economy class or not. European airlines (and you may end up on a European airline if you are transiting through Europe, even if you start off on an American airline) have very strict rules about the size, weight, and number of bags you can check or bring on board. Many airlines only allow eight kilograms (17.6 lbs.) for carry-on bags—some bags weigh that much when empty!

South African Airways, the primary airline that flies to destinations in southern Africa, also maintains very strict carry-on rules. This means that you will have to check your bags, even if you normally would want to just have carry-on baggage, which then increases your exposure to the Johannesburg airport's notorious theft problem from checked baggage. Some travelers severely limit their luggage to avoid checking bags and also limit purchases. Others send bags ahead by mail and other services. Some travelers buy clothes and supplies as they need them along the way and leave them behind before they return home. Putting things into perspective, I have had my checked baggage rifled through and things stolen from the San Francisco airport, but not from Johannesburg, so you never know.

Some people plan all of their travel around building up mileage through an airline's frequent flyer program. In the pre-COVID-19 era, airplane seats were oversold and passengers jammed into ever smaller space; few amenities existed anymore. The status that an airline's frequent flyer program affords passengers, according to how many miles they have flown on that carrier, may be the only way to get perks, such as boarding the plane earlier than others. Or it could mean the ability to check your luggage for free. If you only travel a bit and want to sign up for multiple airline frequent flyer programs, most likely you will never amass enough points to raise your status on any of the airlines. But many airlines are part of the same system, such as Star Alliance—that includes United and Lufthansa—which you can leverage to earn a higher status faster. Keep in mind, if you plan to use your accumulated air miles to buy a plane ticket, airlines generally "black out" dates around major holidays, so you can't use your miles for holiday travel. Of course, no one knows what airlines will be like in the post-COVID-19 era.

DISASTERS AND UNREST

Natural disasters usually strike with no or little warning. Think earthquakes, tsunamis, and volcano eruptions. Some may think potential natural disasters may be a reason to avoid overseas travel, but no country is immune. The US also faces earthquakes, tornadoes, hurricanes, or even the occasional volcano, yet we still carry on. So, there is no reason to avoid travel because of this potential risk, but you do want to be informed and prudent. If you know that a volcano has been active lately, you may want to view it from afar. Usually, though, we can't plan travel around potential natural disasters.

More likely, you may run into man-made events. Stay informed through the US Department of State's travel warnings and keep up on international news. These might include strikes, demonstrations, environmental events, or military action. Oftentimes you are given warning—workers in a city will call a general strike, or you hear that people are planning a demonstration. Sometimes a government imposes a curfew, which you should heed especially since security forces, even the military, could be sent out to enforce the curfew.

When the Tiananmen Massacre occurred on June 4, 1989, in the heart of Beijing, people had already been demonstrating since April with the death of Hu Yaobang, former General Secretary of the Chinese Communist Party. Initially, the protests had a festive air, with a show of unity and courtesy between students and workers, groups that usually did not mix. During this "festive" time, many foreign tourists went to Tiananmen Square to observe the demonstrations. Tensions continued to rise until the military cracked down on June 4th, injuring and killing demonstrators. Once the fighting started, tourists stayed in their hotels and away from Tiananmen

Square. As previously mentioned, Susan and I were on a train from the northwest of China to Beijing on June 4th. We could not continue our journey to Beijing, which was closed under martial law, but we finally maneuvered our way out to Hong Kong.

Many people prepare a "go bag" that includes essential items, including your passport and any medications, so that you can pick up the bag and go on the spur of the moment. In the US, we don't tend to prepare this way unless you are pregnant and anticipate needing to rush to the hospital soon. In potentially precarious situations that may require you to leave quickly, it is definitely recommended to have a "go bag" ready.

Bottom line, if you know something is amiss, or potentially amiss, stay away from that area. There usually are other sites to visit.

BRIBES AND OTHER TIPS

You could face the situation where you are asked for a bribe, either overtly or subtly. You will have to evaluate your situation. Is someone just harassing you or telling you he can get something done for you, when in fact you just need to walk up to the ticket counter and purchase your own ticket? Or you could be wandering around the Cairo museum and one of the guards in the exhibit hall will say he can show you something special if you give him a "tip." In these instances, you can usually ignore the person and he will approach the next person instead.

On the other hand, if you are driving and get stopped at a checkpoint as I did once in Albania, you may encounter a policeman who mentions that Christmas is coming and he needs to purchase gifts for his children. You might assess this situation differently. If you are in the middle of nowhere and it is dark, it's probably best to give him some money so that you can be on your way. Or if you are in Moscow and someone tries to mug you, you probably want to hand over some money.

Then there's tipping. Tipping is a complicated situation, depending on where you are in the world. As an American, you are used to tipping at restaurants, in taxis, and at salons, but overseas it can be different. In many places in Europe, you just round up your bill instead of leaving a tip, which makes me (and other Americans) feel uncomfortable. There are plenty of guides out there to research tipping in the country you will visit.[103] And some countries don't expect you to tip at all.[104] I always try to figure out tipping before I travel.

If you are in a place where tipping is acceptable and someone really is doing you a favor, you can provide a tip to show your appreciation. Once I was working on a project in Cairo and we needed to move into new office space. We decided to do so on a Saturday, so it was less disruptive, but the elevator man did not work on Saturdays. We needed him to run the elevator, though. So, we provided him with a tip so that he could come in and operate the elevator on his day off.

From tipping we move to beggars, who can be found in many parts of the world. Depending on how you view beggars, they can be quite upsetting, such as what I encountered in Kabul. Some women in burqas sit in the middle of the street, a blue blob with outstretched hands beseeching for help from the cars weaving around them, a heartbreaking

103 "Tips on Gratuity: To Tip or Not to Tip around the World," *Currencyfair* (blog), January 3, 2017.

104 Jenny Horowitz, "Tipping around the World: A Global Gratuity Guide," *Western Union\\WU* (blog), July 31, 2017.

scene to witness. Children will also approach you in Kabul, small and dirty, and you feel sorry for them. On my first trip there I traveled with an Afghan-American colleague. She adamantly refused to give the children money; she said that if we did so, they would get used to it and would continue to beg. This is an argument you will also hear of panhandlers and the homeless in the US, and sometimes it is hard to know what is the "right" thing to do.

And then there is bargaining. Often in the developing world, you need to bargain when buying things. Of course, you need to know when it is appropriate—usually you won't barter in stores, but sometimes you can; you almost always barter if you are in an outdoors market. There are all sorts of tips on how best to barter; I include some that I use here:

- First, you need to look disinterested.
- Then, when you finally decide to show some interest, you should offer no more than half of what the vendor is quoting. So, if he says something costs fifty dollars, then you should start at twenty-five dollars, if not less.
- They often will tell you a song and dance story about how they are giving you a deal because you are their first customer, or their last customer, or their good friend, or whatever.
- Beware—it's a game or dance that you must play, and you will eventually end up somewhere in the middle, sometimes with tea involved.
- If you buy more than one item, you have more leverage for a higher discount.

At the end of the day, they depend on this livelihood, probably supporting an extended family. I'm not a ruthless bargainer, but I know others who are and take great pride in getting the lowest price, even though the differences may be small and the price is often affordable to us. If it isn't, you can always walk away.

In places like Manila, Philippines, and sometimes in Washington, DC, when you stop your car at a traffic light, someone will approach your vehicle and start washing your windshield, even if you don't want this service. Then you are in a bind as they have already washed the window, so you feel you should give them some money. In other places, such as in Mozambique for cars and in Cambodia for motorcycles, people will help guide you into a parking space and "watch" over your car or motorcycle while you are in the store or restaurant. These "car parkers" are usually just random people who have "taken over" that section of the curb. It's always good to pay them some money when you return to your car or motorcycle, as they have watched over it while you were gone and kept away any thieves.

On a separate note, if you throw away any written notes, receipts, or documents before departure from your hotel, you should always rip up the papers. Depending on where you are, cleaning staff may retrieve your papers to reuse somehow—sometimes to use as wrapping materials, or maybe even to make shoes. I've even had a cleaning staff ask if she could have the pantyhose I was throwing away.

And oftentimes when I travel, I leave t-shirts or shorts behind when I return home. I also usually carry a stack of books with me (yes, I prefer books) and leave them along the way as I finish reading them. I figure the staff can either use them or sell them, and it allows room for purchases I may make on my travels!

KEEPING YOUR TEMPER IN CHECK

Traveling anywhere in the world, even in the US, can try your patience. You can lose your temper and take it out on people who are just trying to do their job. Or you can take things in stride—there is nothing you can really do, so why waste your energy on getting mad? Or you can be like the Chinese, who laugh in the face of adversity.

In my experience, unless you are in immediate danger, it is better to remain calm and try to look at things rationally with a strong dose of humor than to resort to anger and shouting. If you are dealing with an airline personnel, remember that his stress level is up as flights are being canceled and hundreds of people are trying to rebook their flights. If you show the person some empathy and seek their assistance, you may find that they respond much better to you than to the person who is shouting at them. Here is a piece of advice for when your flight is delayed, at least in the US—while you should get in line to change your flight, you should also call the airlines. Your call may actually get through before you make it to the head of the line. But don't get me wrong, sometimes there is a place to get mad and demand something happens. You need to play this by ear, although it's hard to turn anger on and off.

BE PREPARED

Prepare...you never know what you will encounter. Walking back from dinner in a Shenyang (the capital of China's Liaoning Province) neighborhood in the dead of winter, Susan had to use the bathroom. In China, at that time, the communal public toilets were basically buildings over open trenches, and to be avoided at all costs. In this case, Susan realized she could not wait and bravely took her chances in the darkened building. I waited outside. I waited and waited and waited—one Chinese woman went in and came out and then another. I was beginning to wonder when finally, Susan came out. She said, "I never realized how hard it is to pull your pants down with many layers of clothes on, squat and aim properly, and then dig out your Kleenex and protect your camera, all in the dark." Evidently, Chinese women were much more adept at this, but they also weren't carrying cameras with them!

It is a good rule to always have Kleenex with you when using the facilities. And don't be surprised if you find a hole for a toilet. Depending on the situation, these actually can be more hygienic than some sit-down toilets, but they are tricky if you are not used to squatting. In some places, toilet paper will clog up the sewage pipes, so if there's a pail with used, crumpled tissue in it, place your used paper in the pail. Sometimes there's a fee for use of the toilet. When President Clinton visited the Great Wall of China, no one told the Chinese attendant collecting latrine fees what the President looked like. She wasn't going to let him get by without paying half a cent, which got him three sheets of toilet paper.

Sometimes it's best to ask questions. I traveled upcountry in Liberia once and we stayed at a small hotel. When we checked in, I noted that each room had its own bathroom with running water and a bucket to wash. The next morning when I got up to take a shower, I turned the tap on, and nothing came out! I had to make do with a small bottle of drinking water. When I came down for breakfast, I commented on how there was no water. My coworkers laughed and told me that everyone knew you needed to fill up the bucket the night before, as the water would run out by morning. Who knew?

SAFETY AND SECURITY

But other things can happen that can affect your safety and security. For example, car accidents are always a potential danger. Many cars don't have seat belts and the driver's capabilities are sometimes questionable. Moreover, emergency medical services for victims of a car crash can be limited. I have known people to exit a taxi after realizing there were no seat belts available.

You can be especially susceptible to getting sick while traveling. There are a number of reasons you can be vulnerable: flying long distances in airplanes with the germs being recycled, being exhausted from the flight and jet lag reducing your ability to fight illness, being exposed to contaminants and bacteria you may not be adapted to, lack of refrigeration or hygienic handling of foods, etc. As discussed in Chapter 3, in some countries, you need to be very careful about what you eat and drink—even in nice hotels you may have problems. I experienced my worst stomach sickness after eating fresh grapes in a five-star hotel in Cairo.

Prior to traveling, there are a number of places to get good information, including the US Department of State's webpage for travelers that provides information on medical precautions, safety, scams, and evacuation insurance.[105] Consult the CDC for medical information, including immunizations or malaria prophylaxis you may need.[106] You will also want to enroll in the State Department's Smart Traveler Enrollment Program (STEP) to receive travel alerts, to ensure that the State Department will know how to contact you in an

---

105 US Department of State, Bureau of Consular Affairs, *MyTravelGov*, accessed September 3, 2020.

106 Centers for Disease Control and Prevention, *Traveler's Health*, accessed September 3, 2020.

emergency, and to designate in advance which of your family or friends State may give information to about your welfare and whereabouts should anything happen while you're traveling.[107] Non-Americans will likely have similar resources from their own country.

On your travels, you always need to be aware of your surroundings and keep tabs on your bags and luggage. When you arrive at some airports in developing countries, such as in Abuja, Nigeria, people will try to grab at your luggage to "help" you with them. It's best not to let them do so. Backpacks, while convenient, are ripe pickings for thieves, so be careful, especially in crowded public transportation stations or aboard trains and buses. Thieves are prevalent in crowded spaces, especially where tourists congregate. Some of them can be very sophisticated, like the time we were robbed in Paris by two people who said they were the police—they weren't. There can also be gangs of robbers in some European cities that may look like a family or group of homeless women and children but are actually well-coordinated and skilled in pickpocketing. If they come near you with a newspaper over their arm, beware.

Some luggage companies have backpacks, purses, and fanny packs that include slash proof material and wire reinforced straps. While these bags may be more expensive than regular bags, they provide some sense of peace of mind that you have now made it harder for a thief to target you.

If you do get your passport stolen or have another emergency while overseas, call your nearest embassy or consulate. Always carry a photocopy of your passport and any current

---

107 US Department of State, Bureau of Consular Affairs, *Smart Traveler Enrollment Program (STEP)*, accessed September 3, 2020.

visa stamped inside your passport in a separate location in case your passport gets stolen or you lose it. Also, research whether your destination country requires you to carry your passport with you when you are in-country.

If you travel to places like Afghanistan or Iraq, you won't be doing so on your own, it's too dangerous. Usually, you will be going for work and be met by someone from your host organization at the airport. Your host organization will have security protocols in place which you must follow. Depending on the country, they may provide you with a way to track where you are and provide body armor and access to a safe room.

In many developing countries, you will want to arrange transportation from the airport to your hotel beforehand, either with your host organization or with the hotel directly. Some places like Maputo, Mozambique, may not have reliable taxis, while to get to the center of Bangkok you can take the airport rail link, a taxi, or airport limos. Read up before you depart to see what the situation is. When I recently traveled to Frankfurt, where I had not been in a long time, I researched that the easiest and cheapest way to my hotel from the airport was to take the light rail. A colleague ran out of time to research this and took a taxi to the hotel, which cost a lot more.

Depending on where you are traveling, "fixers" may become your best friend. Drivers are often the ones who play this crucial role. They help keep their clients safe, serve as tour guides and cross-cultural awareness instructors, and they can help get you out of a jam. Hotel concierges are also a good source of information and can help you get tickets, put you in contact with drivers and others who can help, and provide recommendations for restaurants and other places to visit. If you are traveling for work, ask your client or coworkers for recommendations. I would not trust someone who randomly targets you on the street and suggests he can show you around.

CULTURE SHOCK

Beware, culture shock can hit you at any time, even when you have returned to the US. Everyone does things differently, whether you are in the US or overseas. Oftentimes, there is no right or wrong way to do something, it's just different. Some Asians may slurp their soup noodles to show their appreciation while Americans think it rude. Americans use serving spoons while Chinese use their chopsticks to pick food up from a communal dish. Many cultures use their hands to eat.

You can easily identify these examples as potential triggers for culture shock. But it's when culture shock sneaks up on you, causing you to have an outburst or break down into tears—that's when you are surprised. Whether you are moving overseas or on a short trip, culture shock can hit you five days or three months into your stay, usually after the newness and the "honeymoon" is over and reality sets in. Just remember that this is normal, and to take some deep breaths or a few minutes by yourself to clear your mind. This is a temporary situation, then you can get back to exploring and enjoying your trip.

I once traveled with a small group that was crossing the Chinese-Hong Kong border in 2012. Our Chinese bus took us to the border. We off-loaded our luggage and walked up to the Chinese passport control. We then walked across the border and went through the Hong Kong passport control, all the while toting our luggage. Once through the second passport control, we came out of the building and boarded a different bus on the Hong Kong side. We were all hot, exhausted, and eager to get to our Hong Kong hotel to rest. Suddenly, one woman in our group had an uncharacteristic meltdown that lasted several minutes about why we had to do this and why they couldn't just drive us across the border. She eventually recovered, embarrassed, while the rest of the group took it all in stride. This was just the way it was, and no amount of yelling or screaming would alleviate the process. If anything, it may have slowed us down. We all had a meltdown at least once during the trip, even if we did not have an outburst.

Culture shock often manifests itself when you are tired or not feeling well. That's when you want things to be like they are at home, and you don't have the patience to deal with things being done differently. When you feel that you are getting frustrated with how things are being done, try to take a break, some deep breaths, a walk, a nap, or whatever else that will help you be able to look at things more objectively again.

WRAP-UP

This chapter isn't meant to scare you, it's meant to get you thinking about preparing for potential adversity. Much of it relies on planning and common sense. You wouldn't go down that dark alley at home, so you won't do that overseas either. More often than not, bad things don't happen. But if you aren't sure about something, just ask! It's better to ask than to wake up to no water. And as Epictetus, the Greek Stoic philosopher, said, "It's not what happens to you, but how you react to it that matters."[108]

---

108 Goodreads, "Epictetus > Quotes," accessed September 3, 2020.

Next up, let's see how you can travel from your own living room!

CHAPTER 8

TRAVEL FROM YOUR OWN LIVING ROOM

———

JOANNE'S STORY

Washington, DC is an international city filled with diplomats and others from around the world, as well as those who travel for work or pleasure. Most of our close friends either work under USAID-funded projects or directly for USAID, the US military, or the US Department of State. But many Americans have never traveled, often because they don't have the resources, they don't have the time to do so, or they have no desire.

Joanne Galloway, a native Michigander whom I met when our company had an office in the Upper Peninsula (UP) of Michigan, is one such person. She raised her three children with her husband, Gary, on a farm in the Eastern UP. While she lived thirty miles from the international border with Canada, she has never been internationally focused, and has only visited Canada a handful of times when they lived in Pickford. She grew up in a rural area but received her bachelor's degree from Michigan's Grand Valley State

University before deciding to return to farming. Joanne, a very down-to-earth and pragmatic farmer, weathered the ups and downs of running a farm and raising their children, whom she homeschooled for a time. While never having had political ambitions, Joanne decided to run for Michigan's 107th House district in 2018. Unfortunately, she lost, but that experience galvanized her to focus on grassroots issues that are important to the people of northern Michigan.

When asked if she had a desire to travel overseas, she stated, "We did just sell the farm, where I've been tied down for twenty years making it hard to travel. Now, without that responsibility, travel is very high on our list. But while I am very open to it, I don't know how I will like traveling."

This hesitancy about travel doesn't extend to how Joanne and Gary raised their children. "We taught them to never be afraid of anything." So, they supported trips for their children to Paris, Berlin, Italy, Cuba, Guatemala, and Costa Rica. And Joanne and Gary "love going to ethnic restaurants," and they "both enjoy trying new things." Yet when pressed about traveling overseas, Joanne raised concerns about not knowing where to go or how to communicate. So, she's taking it slowly with their first trip planned for Puerto Rico.

But at the same time, she can provide advice to others who travel. Joanne learned that her friend was flying to Florida for the first time with her boyfriend and her children, and that she was deferring decisions to the boyfriend. Dismayed, Joanne offered, "You want to travel with your kids in a way that they're learning how to travel so that they'll be prepared to travel without you one day, they'll know how you figured it out, they'll know how you looked at the ticket on your phone and knew where to go." This advice came from Joanne's own domestic travel experience as well as how she encouraged her own children to travel on their own.

Joanne finds the thought of overseas travel daunting and doesn't even know where to begin. She realizes that it will require a lot of research online to figure out where to go. This is completely the opposite problem that citizens of the world face—we want to visit so many places, we can't decide where to go to first. Joanne looks forward to reading a book that discusses countries and includes stories and anecdotes about differences in customs, food, and how to interact with local people. "I think it'd be very interesting to read, especially from the perspective of somebody who's got a lot of travel experience and has written from their firsthand stories."

As she and Gary continue trying ethnic restaurants in their new home in Michigan's capital, Lansing, they may catch the travel bug. Joanne commented, "Who knows, since I like exploring new places, once I start traveling overseas, I might enjoy it and want to continue." But in the meantime, they will continue to make forays into other cultures through food and cultural events right from their own backyard.

WHAT IF I'VE NEVER OR RARELY TRAVELED OVER-SEAS?

As this book has demonstrated, traveling overseas provides you with different experiences than you will find at home, and it also highlights our common humanity. Maya Angelou sums it up nicely: "Perhaps travel cannot prevent bigotry, but by demonstrating that all peoples cry, laugh, eat, worry, and die, it can introduce the idea that if we try and understand each other, we may even become friends."[109]

Some people never get a chance to leave their hometown due to financial, professional, or personal reasons, but they still dream and "travel" overseas from their armchairs. Some know that one day they want to travel, so they want to prepare ahead of time. Others need to travel for work. Some want their children to be exposed to different worlds and cultures. Some may only hope to travel one day. Whether to prepare for a trip overseas or just to learn more about the world, you can research a lot from home, made all the simpler by access to the internet.

Whatever the reason, you can now start to build your knowledge of foreign cultures and become a citizen of the world right from your own living room, even if you live in a one-stop-sign town. Some activities will be more accessible than others, but you can also plan a trip to a nearby city to participate in events that may not be readily available locally. Good sites that you can use to look for internationally-focused cultural events, as well as documentaries that you can view from home, are the Smithsonian Institution—and its affiliated Smithsonian Associates—and the National Geographic Society.

Some people have not traveled because they have fears of the unknown, the language barrier, or the potential to be robbed, to name a few reasons.[110] Yes, it can be scary, but if you prepare, you have already positioned yourself in a better

---

109 Goodreads, "Maya Angelou > Quotes > Quotable Quote," accessed September 5, 2020.

110 Dejan Kvrgic, "Fear of Travel: 11 Fears That Stop You from Traveling," *Lifehack* (blog), accessed September 5, 2020.

place, and the more you travel, the more comfortable you will find it to be.[111]

WHAT IF I CAN'T TRAVEL OVERSEAS?

Seasoned travelers, on the other hand, find it almost painful when they don't have an upcoming trip planned. To fill the void, we eat at ethnic restaurants, attend cultural events from foreign lands, or watch foreign films. And many of us consider ourselves lifelong learners and will continue to study and experience new cultural activities even at home. If you live in a major city, these types of opportunities proliferate. Susan and I are lucky to live in the Washington, DC area as international cultural events, as well as geopolitical discussions, occur all the time. Many of these are events that are recorded and available online, so you, too, can watch from home.

I definitely get the itch when I have not traveled overseas for a while. To keep myself sane, I created a book club focused on international books and an international food group that selects a different ethnic restaurant each month. I have considered forming an international film group, but we haven't created that yet. Whenever a local museum features an internationally-focused exhibit, we schedule a visit. During the COVID-19 pandemic, when overseas travel virtually came to a halt, my fellow citizens of the world and I started going stir-crazy, as was manifested in our social media posts as we "traveled" from the living room to the kitchen to the porch.

If you live in small cities or rural areas, there are still plenty of things you can do. You can usually dine at ethnic

---

111 Amanda Williams, "The World Is Not Safe – but You Should Explore It Anyway." *A Dangerous Business Travel Blog.* December 21, 2018.

restaurants, meet immigrants in your community, and learn about other cultures through a local university or library. And with the internet, not only can you research about the world, but you can also watch foreign films and documentaries, visit museums, and listen to world music. This chapter highlights potential opportunities.

Dive into another culture—the more uncomfortable or foreign an experience, the more you will get out of it. This could pertain to jumping into the culture of another country, or it could be going to a rock concert with your son and experiencing a whole new "foreign" culture right in your neighborhood.

RESTAURANTS

The easiest way to start learning about a different culture is to see what restaurants are in your hometown. "Ethnic" restaurants, whether Chinese, Thai, Greek, or Lebanese, for example, dot the American landscape. Be adventuresome; what can it hurt? If you don't like it, you'll know not to order it next time. You can always start off by ordering something familiar, like chicken and vegetables, and expand from there.

I know it is easy to fall into a rut and return to your favorite restaurant to order your favorite dish. I am guilty of that as well. Sometimes I arrive at a restaurant and plan on ordering something new…only to realize I ordered the same dishes again! One way to expand your repertoire of dishes is to share with your dining partner(s). Instead of each person ordering their own dish, everyone orders a different dish and then you all share.

You can also look for other local opportunities. Will there be a local Christmas bazaar featuring one or more ethnic groups you can attend? What a perfect and easy way to expand your horizons. Can you ask someone from a different ethnicity for restaurant recommendations? Or better yet, can you have that person come with you to dinner, or ask them to teach you how to cook something from their home country?

In the Washington, DC area, you can find many Ethiopian restaurants. This may sound familiar to you...I hesitated to go to Ethiopian restaurants, as I didn't know what to order. I could read about the food before going to the restaurant, or ask the server for suggestions, but I still wasn't comfortable. Finally, an Ethiopian friend suggested we dine at an Ethiopian restaurant, and I jumped at the chance. I found the food delicious, even the *kitfo*, or ground raw beef. I normally do not eat raw beef, although I like my beef medium rare, but my friend told me how good it is and how everyone in Ethiopia eats it. I decided to try it and was glad I did. While Ethiopian will not be my first choice when asked where I want to go to (I am partial to Italian and Chinese), if friends suggest we go to an Ethiopian restaurant, I now have broken the "fear" factor and will gladly accept the invitation.

Interestingly, I will eat certain foods while in an "ethnic" context that I normally do not eat. The raw beef is one example. Another example is coffee, which I take black. When I am at a Middle Eastern restaurant, I will order Arabic coffee with sugar. Or I will eat reindeer in Finland and pounded yam in Ghana. Somehow, I justify that if another culture eats something a certain way, I should follow suit.

Some ethnic groups congregate in certain cities and their restaurants proliferate. In some cities you can find Chinatowns, Koreatowns, and Japantowns. Chicago is known for Polish food; New York for Italian, although you can probably get any type of food you want there; New Orleans for Cajun; Tex-Mex in Texas; and Middle Eastern in Michigan. When you travel domestically, check out restaurant options you can try that are different from those at home.

At most ethnic restaurants, the servers happily answer questions about the menu and suggest dishes that fit your tastes. They may even offer to leave out an ingredient you don't like, such as bamboo shoots, make a dish less spicy, or make you a dish that is not on the menu.

We all have fears of the unfamiliar, but dining in a local "ethnic" restaurant provides a safe and fun way to experience something new. Make a plan to visit all the ethnic restaurants in your town. Then you can figure out your favorite ones.

ETHNIC COOKING

In addition to ethnic restaurants, cooking classes, cookbooks, and recipes abound these days to help you cook different foods.

Through television, DVDs from your public library, or YouTube, you can find cooking classes for every ethnic type of food imaginable. They take you step-by-step through the entire process of cooking a dish. You can also buy cookbooks, or your library may carry some. Additionally, you can search for recipes online and find one for almost any dish.

A local community center or store may offer ethnic cooking classes that you can attend. What about ingredients, you ask? Even in some of the smallest towns, often the local grocery store has a small international section where you can find things like soy sauce, dried noodles, and chili sauce, as well as ingredients for Mexican food. If not, there is always the internet, where you can purchase almost anything you need. Sometimes you may not be able to find all of the ingredients, but if you can get some of the suggested spices or flavorings, your dishes will already taste different.

Owen Goslin moved back to Cheboygan, Michigan, in 2016 with his wife, Shihoka, who originally hails from Japan. I asked if his family had adjusted to living in northern Michigan, and how they were coping with the food there. He stated that they loved living in Cheboygan, and though they don't have a Japanese restaurant locally, "you can order nori (seaweed) and Japanese rice and all kinds of staples online." So, they can make great Japanese food at home; the only thing they can't purchase online is fish to make sushi.

Interestingly, when you travel overseas, many grocery stores also have an international food section, which includes American foods! Almost all over the world you can find Pringles, Spam, and Snickers bars!

GETTING TO KNOW YOUR OWN FAMILY BACKGROUND

What about your own background? Have you traced your roots to know where your family comes from? This can open up a whole new world for you. For some of us, this is easier than for others; we come from one ethnicity, or our parents or grandparents have immigrated to the US. Some families pass down traditions from the "old" country, others don't. But you can always start now. Many descendants from Scandinavia and Finland live in the Upper Peninsula of Michigan and Minnesota and carry out traditional activities, like eating *lutfisk* (Norwegian and Swedish dried fish), *smorgas* (Swedish open sandwich), or *pulla* (Finnish cardamom bread), or taking a sauna. Each ethnic group passes down family recipes.

Oftentimes, you may think of your family traditions as just that—your family traditions. But exploring them can be very revealing, which can lead to further research into your ethnic background.

As discussed in Chapter 1, my family has its roots in Guangdong, so we only ate Cantonese food, which is lighter and less greasy than other types of Chinese food. But as both sides of my family did not live in Chinatown, we straddled our Chinese heritage and the American world around us. So, we ate Cantonese food, especially for Chinese New Year's Eve or at lunch on Sunday, yet we also often ate spaghetti, meatloaf, and pork chops on other nights. When I was growing up in the San Francisco Bay Area in the 1960s, the majority of Asian restaurants were Cantonese; we didn't have Thai, Burmese, or Malaysian restaurants back then. In fact, I remember once that my parents and I were invited to a "northern Chinese" restaurant. We ate with trepidation—I remember a sizzling rice dish that was new to me—and determined that nothing beat Cantonese food! To this day, my father only likes Cantonese food among all of the different Asian cuisines available now in the US.

Susan's family is of Finnish ethnicity. She remembers as a child taking saunas at friends' and relatives' houses and afterwards enjoying Finnish coffee, a social time focused on eating the many things on the ladened table: all types of baked breads, cheeses, meats, and, of course, coffee. She also remembers making *viili*, a traditional Finnish yogurt.

Continuing your family traditions is always a great way to learn more about a particular ethnicity. I highly recommend exploring your heritage, which will be a fun way to expand your knowledge of other cultures.

CULTURAL ACTIVITIES

Beyond food, you should take advantage of cultural events that come to your town. This could take the form of an exhibit at a museum, a music group, or a festival. If you are interested in a particular country, plan a trip to a city when they are having an exhibit at the art museum or a special performance featuring that country. Oftentimes, other cultural events for that same country are planned around the exhibit.

Or your hometown may have a local club that features a particular ethnic group that hosts cultural events.

The internet provides a much easier way to find out what may be happening, and it's also a good place to learn about the cultural aspects of a country. Museums will have overviews and highlights of their collections online, and there is YouTube and other video sites where you can learn about other cultures or listen to international music.

Books, books, books…including history books, guidebooks, memoirs, novels, and picture books, all available at your bookstore, library, or via the internet. There are dense books filled with facts and figures, and there are fast reads. Pick a country, or a city, or read about all sorts of places in the world. You can also access book reviews, whether they be professional ones from a newspaper or radio show, or the ones done by readers like you online. A few of my favorite books include:

- China – *Postcards from Tomorrow Square: Reports from China*, James Fallows
- Vietnam – *The Eaves of Heaven: A Life in Three Wars*, Andrew X. Pham
- The Middle East – *A Peace to End All Peace: The Fall of the Ottoman Empire and the Creation of the Modern Middle East*, David Fromkin
- Kenya – *The Challenge for Africa*, Wangari Maathai
- Italy – *Under the Tuscan Sun: At Home in Italy*, Frances Mayes

- The Balkans – *Balkan Ghosts: A Journey Through History*, Robert D. Kaplan

Fiction may offer you vivid and memorable stories that add emotional insight into family relationships, social hierarchy, deep-seated values and beliefs, or generational change. I especially like murder mysteries that take place in foreign lands. Some fiction favorites are:

- Sweden – *The Girl with the Dragon Tattoo*, Stieg Larsson
- Spain – *Shadows of the Pomegranate Tree*, Tariq Ali
- The Middle East – *Women of Sand and Myrrh*, Hanan al-Shaykh
- Nigeria – *Things Fall Apart*, Chinua Achebe
- Japan – *Memoirs of a Geisha*, Arthur Golden
- Chile – *The House of the Spirits*, Isabel Allende

Just read, often and widely.

Like books, movies are also more readily available. Previously, foreign movies could only be viewed at theaters specializing in independent, arty films. Now through Amazon Prime, Netflix, and Hulu, for example, you can readily view foreign movies, American movies about foreign places, or documentaries. Many museums also show foreign movies. Cable channels, or your local public broadcasting station, air foreign movies or travel and foods shows, all of which are cheap ways to travel to a foreign country.

Periodically, lists are put out about the best books on… you name the country or city. Or lists of best movies, such as *The 50 Best Travel Films of All Time*, are issued.[112] You can access so much from your own living room now!

GETTING TO KNOW YOUR NEIGHBORS

How about your own community? Even in some of the smallest towns, you may have community members who hail from a different country (or maybe even a different part of the US) who adhere to a different religion or culture. To expand your global acumen, find ways to get to know these families who can impart knowledge about their country and culture. As with any new family on the block, take it slow and get to know them first. Potential ways to meet foreigners include participating in community centers or events, volunteering to tutor in English or computer skills, or being a patron to merchants and restaurants. As you share information and knowledge about your local community to them, they will begin to open up and share information about where they came from. Maybe they will eventually invite you to participate in one of their holiday celebrations, or to a wedding or birth of a child.

When I was growing up, our neighbors across the street were originally from Italy. They were always eating Italian food, with lots of garlic and freshly made Italian bread! It always smelled so good at their house. And friends of my grandparents were *nisei*, children born of Japanese immigrants. Every New Year's Day, they invited my grandparents to their traditional Japanese buffet.

Whether at work, at the PTA, or at a committee you might serve on, in this day and age of globalization, the likelihood

112 "The 50 Best Travel Films of All Time," *Conde Nast Traveler*, March 16, 2020.

that there will be one or more "foreigners" in your group is high. Volunteering to work on such groups provides you with the opportunities to work with people from other cultures.

Your workplace may also expose you to a multicultural environment, either with your coworker down the hall, or your company may have offices in other parts of the world. Getting to know these global actors can enhance your work relationships, but also introduce you to your coworker's culture and country.

You can also encourage local schools to hold an International Day where all the countries represented in the school share things about their native cultures. Or each culture can celebrate their special holiday as it is celebrated throughout the year. As I previously mentioned, in elementary school I was obligated to discuss Chinese New Year; bringing fortune cookies each year for my classmates was fun! Schools can also promote international potluck days where students volunteer to bring a dish from a specific country, providing them the opportunity to visit an international grocery store or try a new recipe.

CLASSES OR STUDY OPPORTUNITIES

Another way to learn about different cultures is through classes in a nearby college, adult education facility, public library, or even specialized clubs. These classes could be on history, language, cooking, or culture. If the teacher is from the country you are studying, find ways to interact with that person to learn more than just what is being presented. They may even have a network of people that they can introduce you to, either locally or if you travel to their country. Online classes are another great way to learn new things.

As you think about overseas travel, you can also incorporate "learning" into a vacation. Some programs offer opportunities where you can go to study the language and culture in a foreign country for a couple of weeks or longer, sometimes even affording the opportunity to live with a local family during your stay. This provides an excellent way to get to know the culture better, as well as to continuously have opportunities to practice the language. You will really get to know how the locals live and be able to eat homecooked food!

Organizations such as American Field Service (now known as AFS-USA), Youth for Understanding, or Rotary International, sponsor exchange programs. Hosting an exchange student provides your family an opportunity to jump-start your knowledge of another country. The programs usually last for an academic year or a summer. Be prepared to both impart information about our culture to the student, while also learning about their culture. Some exchange programs are only a week long, but a lot can be learned in even just a week.

Likewise, encourage your children to go abroad under one of these exchange programs. Some high schools also organize tours overseas, often to Europe. If you can afford this, the exposure your child receives on an exchange program or a tour will begin the process of making him or her comfortable in the global environment. As a high school friend, Jane Lande Nick, reflected about her time as an exchange student in Germany, "It was a life changing experience. It made me appreciate the US and understand cultural differences."

As mentioned, I participated in a summer Youth for Understanding program to Zurich, Switzerland, when I was in high school. It was quite an experience, not knowing anyone and arriving to live with a family for two months.

My Swiss family had two sons that were older than me, and they lived in the city (I grew up in a suburb), so I learned how to use public transportation to get around. With my Swiss brothers, I participated in an anti-nuclear protest march and traveled to southern Switzerland where we camped alongside a river, moving into a barn when it started raining in the middle of the night. This experience posed challenges but also was eye-opening to a different culture for me and piqued my interest in travel.

During college, I participated in an exchange program between UCLA and Zhongshan University in Guangzhou, China, in 1982. Not only did I interact with the Chinese at the university, but I also was able to travel to other parts of China during vacations. I found the experience so worthwhile that I extended it by a year to solidify my Chinese language skills and learn more about China.

Countries participating in exchange programs or overseas tours can reflect changes in the geopolitical environment. For example, China, a closed society for many years, only reopened to the West in 1979. However, less than thirty-five years later, a large group of elementary school aged Chinese came in for dinner at a small Chinese restaurant in Northern Virginia while we were dining. Due to China's restrictions on travel and the lack of disposable income of its citizenry, the likelihood that these students hailed from China was low—I guessed they were from Taiwan. But after speaking to some of them, I found they were from Sichuan Province in China—not only was I surprised that they were from China, but Sichuan is an inland province and had less interaction with the West. How times had changed that these Chinese students were now in the Washington, DC area on a study tour.

KEEP UP ON INTERNATIONAL NEWS

Don't forget about the news. Through the internet and television, you can easily tune into international news and programs. With globalization, the world is really a smaller place, so what happens in one corner of the world may have ramifications globally, as demonstrated by the Black Lives Matter protests in 2020, which started in the US, but then spread to other parts of the world.

As previously discussed, my parents and I traveled to New Zealand and stayed at a bed and breakfast on a wapiti farm on the South Island. The basic bed and breakfast provided the opportunity to see wapiti up close and to interact with local farmers, sharing dinner and breakfast with them. As this was not long after the US presidential election of 2000, we spent time talking about US politics. These simple farmers demonstrated a higher level of understanding of the US than we had, and we knew very little about New Zealand politics.

SURFING THE WEB — A NEW FLYING CARPET

Today anyone can get on their own flying carpet and take off for all four corners of the earth. You can search for information on a country, including the customs, the business environment, the people, the language, the food, the religion, and the history.

For example, you can decide that you want to research *plov*, a rice dish from Uzbekistan. Things that can come up include:

- Food in Uzbekistan, the ingredients of *plov*, and recipes to make it yourself
- Beverages that are common in Uzbekistan
- Family culture

- The different peoples of Uzbekistan
- The Silk Road and the Central Asian crossroads
- How *plov* is also found in other Central Asian countries
- The history of Uzbekistan, including when it was part of the Soviet Union
- The rich religious culture and the architecture spawned from it
- The music of Uzbekistan
- Uzbekistan's connection to Alexander the Great
- The Great Game (the rivalry between the British and Russians over Central Asia in the 19th century)[113]
- And on and on it goes.

As noted above, you can purchase special spices and ingredients not available in your hometown online (you can actually search for Uzbek spices on Amazon). So even though you are thousands of miles from Uzbekistan, you could decide to cook an Uzbek meal one weekend and dine with Uzbek music playing in the background.

WRAP-UP

Whether you are a seasoned traveler or have never left your hometown, you can take advantage of foreign opportunities right from your living room. You can meet different peoples, attend cultural events, dine on ethnic cuisines, or research geopolitical issues. Just because you may not have the opportunity or resources to travel the world currently, if your interest in the world is piqued, one day you may have the chance to board a plane and jet off on an adventure of your own.

---

113 Kallie Szczepanski, "What Was the Great Game?" *ThoughtCo.* (blog), July 31, 2019.

When people ask Dana Vierra—the young history teacher who loves to travel that I previously mentioned—where they should travel to first, she responds, "Just rip the band-aid off and go, it's not as scary as you think. Even if you go with a tour group you will experience something exciting and once you've tasted that forbidden fruit, there's no stopping you." We should all provide such advice to those new to international travel.

And whether you travel from your own living room or venture overseas, remember what Associate Justice of the US Supreme Court Oliver Wendell Holmes, Jr. noted: "A mind that is stretched by a new experience can never go back to its old dimensions."[114]

Next up, some final thoughts.

114 PassItOn, "Oliver Wendell Holmes," accessed September 5, 2020.

FINAL THOUGHTS

For those of you who have not traveled much, I hope that one day you get the chance to travel overseas. Whether your spouse or friends get you to join them on a trip, or your boss calls to tell you to pack your bags as she needs you to jet off to Timbuktu for two weeks, you may find that suddenly you are faced with both fear and excitement! Depending on the amount of your previous overseas travel and where you are now headed, you will experience different levels of unease or anxiety. You are now going somewhere different where you can meet new people, see new things, and experience new foods. Take advantage of the opportunities, and remember, you will be able to return home shortly. After reading this book, you should be more comfortable in the global arena.

I used to think that to be a citizen of the world one had to experience internationally-focused events and travel from an early age, but as I talked to people about this book, I realized that some did have this in their background, but others didn't. A lot of people start out in some part of the US, Asia, Africa, or Latin America, yet they develop an interest and passion to live in the global world. Through my travels, I have become keenly aware of how critical it is to respect and engage people from around the world. It's through people-to-people encounters that we learn. This leads us to expand our outlook to include others who are different from us, which not only enhances our ability to solve problems and deal with global crises, but also reveals our common humanity.

But actually, becoming a citizen of the world is like becoming skilled in anything. To become a violinist, you start from scratch and you study, ask questions, learn from your mistakes, practice, and keep going—and eventually you succeed. You may not become a professional violinist, but you will be comfortable going about it. And remember, being a citizen of the world is not a destination, it's a mindset and a journey.

Those of us who love to hop on a plane to anywhere at any time also can have our moments of anxiety, such as wondering if this taxi driver is really taking me to my destination, or if I will finally end up as one of those statistics you read about. Or we have made mistakes, sometimes knowingly, other times unknowingly, either later to be told or to never know. Traveling outside your home country is both exciting and scary at times. But preparing ahead of time, such as using a tool like my preparation framework, being aware of your surroundings, and interacting with the local population in a friendly manner, will help you feel more at ease with your travels.

And if something just doesn't feel right, then remove yourself from that situation, or decide not to do something. I have still not visited St. Petersburg because I was not comfortable taking the overnight train alone from Moscow to St. Petersburg during a time when thieves were frequently breaking into sleeping compartments while you slept. It's better to not do something and be safe than to put yourself in a potentially dicey position. Meanwhile, other people take risks all the time—you need to do what feels right for you.

Learning to become comfortable in the world, whether you are a tourist, a businessperson who travels internationally periodically, or an expatriate who lives for years away from your own country, is achievable. But there are certain attributes that will help you succeed, such as:

- Curiosity, open-mindedness, and an eagerness to learn
- Respect and empathy for others who are different
- Adaptability and flexibility
- Risk-taking and boldness
- Active listening and relationship building
- A sense of humor and patience

I think one of the important things to think about is the "tone" you set in regards to your attitude, how you act, what you write, and what you say. You need to be authentic and congenial, and know to apologize if you do something wrong, or at least know not to do it again. While you may be apprehensive about traveling, or the meetings you need to attend, try to remain calm about it. Do some research about the country before you go—learn something about the history, the people, the culture, and any issues the country is facing that you should be sensitive about. Learn a few basic words in the local language. Go into a new culture with an open mind and attitude; don't come across as negative, condescending, superior, or aggressive. For citizens of the world, the barriers between us and them are irrelevant and we are people who look at the world comfortably.

To be a successful citizen of the world, one of the theories I recommend studying is the concept of "cultural intelligence" or "CQ."[115] A culturally intelligent person is comprised of three concepts: knowledge or understanding of culture, attention paid to cues from the other party as well as within yourself, and development of skills to react to different cultural situations.[116] After reading books on CQ, I believe that to achieve cultural intelligence is the ultimate goal for those traveling and working in the global environment—it allows one to develop a repertoire of ways to appropriately react in a cross-cultural environment. You may not have in-depth knowledge of a particular culture, but you will be able to become aware of cues that allow you to act accordingly and appropriately. Without being aware of the concept of CQ, I realized that these are the very skills I have developed, and that is what you need to strive for as well if you want to be successful in our global community both abroad and at home.

And for those of you who tend towards introvertedness, don't worry, I'm one of those too. You can still be a global traveler.

I am not sure exactly how I became a citizen of the world, but I know my heritage, my parents' encouragement, and the people I have met along the way—including our wonderful experiences through Untours—have all helped to shape me. I will get on a plane at any time to anywhere. I may not be as adventuresome as some people when it comes to food, nor do I do extreme sports, but I do my best to get as much out of an experience as I can. Who else do you know who hired a driver to look for and find Boris Pasternak's grave, twenty miles from Moscow?

---

115 "About Cultural Intelligence," Cultural Intelligence Center, accessed August 26, 2020.

116 Brooks Peterson, *Cultural Intelligence: A Guide to Working with People from Other Cultures* (Boston: Intercultural Press, 2004), 13.

As former Secretary-General of the United Nations Kofi Annan stated, "We may have different religions, different languages, different colored skin, but we all belong to one human race."[117]

Whether you are a citizen of the world or a novice traveler, I hope to cross paths with you somewhere in the world.

So, where are you going?

---

117 Goodreads, "Kofi Annan> Quotes > Quotable Quote," accessed September 5, 2020.

BONUS MATERIALS: OPERATION PREPARATION

––––––

So, you have your overseas trip scheduled—now what? I've written this section to help you prepare for your trip, gathering information that was discussed in other parts of the book into one convenient place. Please remember that things can change quickly regarding overseas travel. While these tips are up to date at the time of publication, you should double-check things, especially regarding passport and visa requirements, as you get ready for your trip.

The US State Department's webpage for International Travel contains many resources to prepare you.[118] The US Customs and Border Protection also puts out guidance through its "Know Before You Go" guide.[119] A guidebook

––––––

118 US Department of State, Bureau of Consular Affairs, *MyTravelGov: International Travel,* accessed September 3, 2020.

119 US Department of Homeland Security, US Customs and Border Protection, *Know Before You Go,* accessed September 5, 2020.

on the location you are traveling to can help prepare you as well. In summary, I undertake the following preparations.

INITIAL TASKS

Initial Task List

- Passport
- Visa
- Plane reservations
- Hotel reservations
- Travel insurance
- Vaccinations or anti-malaria pills
- Transport from airport to hotel
- Guidebook or other book about the place you are going to

PASSPORTS

Don't forget your passport! You won't be able to get on the plane for an international destination without it. If you have never applied for a passport, you need to allow time to get one.[120]

The US no longer allows US citizens to add blank pages to their passports. Instead, you must renew your passport if you run out of pages. You can request a larger passport book with fifty-two pages at no additional cost when you renew, which is highly recommended if you plan to travel a lot.

---

120 US Department of State, Bureau of Consular Affairs, *MyTravelGov: US Passports,* accessed September 5, 2020.

If you need help, companies known as expediters specialize in helping you obtain a new passport or renew a current passport for a fee. Be mindful of the time, as obtaining the passport, even for a renewal, takes time, with the busiest periods leading up to summer. Normally, the State Department website anticipates six to eight weeks processing time for a routine passport and two to three weeks, plus additional fees, for expedited processing times.

You can also apply for a US Passport Card for an additional fee. You cannot use this card for international air travel, but it can be used when entering the United States at land border crossings and seaport-of-entry from:

- Canada
- Mexico
- The Caribbean
- Bermuda

One advantage of obtaining a US Passport Card is to have a second US State Department-issued identification to expedite getting a new passport if you lose yours overseas.

Some countries require your passport be valid for at least six months and/or you need a certain number of blank pages for the visa. Check the embassy website of the country you are traveling to for their specific passport requirements.

GLOBAL ENTRY AND TSA PRE√®

The US Department of Homeland Security maintains several Trusted Traveler Programs, with Global Entry being the most important for international travelers if you plan on a lot of overseas travel.[121] The Global Entry program expedites the holder through passport control upon re-entry into the US from an overseas trip and includes access to the TSA Pre✓® program, allowing expedited passage through airport security within the US. Currently, the Global Entry fee is one hundred dollars and is valid for five years. Be aware, if you travel with others who don't have Global Entry, they will not be able to accompany you through the expedited line upon arrival back in the US.

VISAS

Each country has different requirements regarding visas. They may exempt travelers from some countries from needing a visa, while others will require it. They may have different types of visas: business, tourist, transit, etc., and they can be single or multiple entry visas. Some visas are only valid for a short period of time, while others can be multi-entry and good for five years. Sometimes you can obtain your visa at the port of entry—be sure to check what the requirements may be. You may need to have cash (sometimes in the local currency, sometimes US dollars are okay) or a passport photo. Sometimes you can complete the application ahead of time. Other countries allow you to obtain a visa online prior to departure.

There are two dates you need to be aware of on a visa. The first date to keep in mind is when the visa expires. This means that you must enter the country prior to the expiration date. The second date is how long you can stay in the country on that visa.

---

121 US Department of Homeland Security, *Trusted Traveler Programs,* accessed September 5, 2020.

When you move to a country, visa requirements will be different. You may need a work permit if you are working or to undergo other registration processes.

Check with the embassy of the country you will visit to learn their visa requirements, or if you are a US citizen, you can check the Country Information webpage at the US State Department website.[122] Expediter companies can help obtain visas too, which may be useful as they know the ins and outs and can reduce the stress—I often use one, especially if I need visas for multiple countries. Allow plenty of time for the visa process.

PLANE RESERVATIONS

Don't forget to buy your plane ticket. Most people purchase their tickets online now, although travel agencies still exist. Each airline has its own website, or there are online companies—such as Expedia and Travelocity—that search multiple airlines, rather than just one. It is challenging to purchase plane tickets now as the prices constantly change, but it is also easy considering that you can see what is available with an internet connection.

Make sure you check the terms and conditions of the ticket you plan on purchasing—it is especially difficult now as some airlines have expanded the types of tickets available. Before, if you were purchasing an economy ticket, there were normally two different types of tickets—refundable (which was more expensive) and non-refundable. Then airlines started adding a different category of economy (like Economy Plus on United) that gave you more leg room. Most

---

122 US Department of State, Bureau of Consular Affairs, *MyTravelGov: International Travel, Country Information*, accessed September 5, 2020.

recently, you have types of tickets that are cheaper but are basically "nothing but the seat." So, make sure you understand what type of ticket you are purchasing.[123]

A note on companies like Expedia and Travelocity: some people use them with no problems. I tend to book directly with the airlines or through a travel agent, especially if I am going overseas. If you have a problem during your trip, such as a flight that has been canceled, it may be difficult to get Expedia to assist you with the rebooking.

If you travel for work, companies handle this differently; some have a centralized travel agency you must use while others let you purchase the ticket from anywhere. Also, are there any restrictions on which airlines you can fly? Projects funded by the US government usually follow the Fly America Act, which requires you to fly on a US airline (or codeshare) to and from the US. Another question is what class of travel are you authorized? Some companies will only pay for economy class, no matter how long the flight. Does your company want you to purchase a non-refundable or refundable ticket? Oftentimes, they want you to purchase a non-refundable ticket because the cost to change the ticket is not that great, relatively speaking.

Other issues to keep in mind include the routing, number of layovers, and what time you will arrive at your destination. Some routings with several layovers extend the length of your flight time, which you will not appreciate if your flight is already long. Several layovers can also increase your anxiety in regards to whether you'll make it in time for your connection, which may be way across to the other side of the airport,

---

123 Ed Perkins, "The 4 Different Types of Economy Airfare, Defined," *Airfarewatchdog* (blog). March 16, 2018.

or even in a different terminal. Other times you may have a choice of transit points—choose carefully. You may want to reconsider transiting through Minneapolis in the middle of winter, due to possible weather delays, if you can go through Atlanta. Some airports are notorious for late departures or strikes. Others may be known for theft. As mentioned in Chapter 7, I once decided to transit through Rome on my way to Albania and had to sit on (very cool-looking) metal mesh chairs, which are quite painful when sitting on them for hours! Of course, sometimes you do not have a choice, but if you do, choose carefully.

Lastly, it is usually better to arrive at your destination during normal hours rather than in the middle of the night. Again, you may not have a choice—flights from the US to the Philippines tend to arrive at 11:00 p.m.

HOTEL RESERVATIONS

Internet searches now make it easy to find lodging, including reading reviews on a particular property. You may stay at known chain hotels, local boutique hotels, Airbnbs, or hostels. I like to stay in local boutique hotels when I travel. There are usually trade-offs between cost of lodging and proximity to the city center or a specific attraction—the closer to the desired location, the more expensive the room. You need to decide if a cheaper room is your priority and you don't care that you may need to take the subway to your hotel in the suburbs. In some locations, such as Washington, DC, lodging on weekends is sometimes cheaper than during the week as business travelers are in Washington during the week and not the weekends.

If you travel for work, ask your local counterparts for hotel suggestions. They will know safe and decent places, and oftentimes they can get you special rates that they have previously negotiated. Your company may use a preferred hotel chain. If you choose the hotel on your own, read up about the area around the hotel for potential red flags in terms of crime and location (you don't want a hotel next to a huge construction zone), as well as to ensure it's near where you need to be for your meetings. In some cities, such as Manila, you do not want to be in a hotel across town from your meeting—that drive could take three hours!

TRAVEL INSURANCE

As you prepare for an overseas trip, check with your health insurance to see if you are covered while overseas.

There are different types of travel insurance you can purchase, such as medical evacuation insurance, medical insurance, or trip cancellation insurance. I tend to usually purchase travel insurance whether I travel for work or pleasure.

VACCINATIONS AND/OR ANTI-MALARIA PILLS

Check with the CDC to see what vaccinations you may need and whether or not you are traveling to an area with malaria.[124] Be aware, there are some countries in Africa and South America where yellow fever is still present, which will require you to have proof of a yellow fever vaccination. The CDC website also has a lot of good information on how to stay healthy while traveling internationally.

---

124 Centers for Disease Control and Prevention, *Traveler's Health*, accessed September 3, 2020.

AIRPORT TO HOTEL TRANSPORTATION

Before you depart, figure out how you will travel from the airport to your hotel. In some locations, such as London, you can take a taxi or hop on the Heathrow Express train. But in other cities, such as Maputo, Mozambique, for security reasons, you do not want to take public transportation (there may be none) or flag a taxi at the airport. Instead, it is better to arrange pick-up and transport through your hotel. Remember to bring a contact number for your hotel in case no one shows up to pick you up at the airport.

PACKING

GENERAL INFORMATION

General Packing List
- Business clothes, if required
- Casual clothes
- Shoes
- Converter, if required
- Plug adaptors
- Medicines
- Small flashlight
- Passport – actual plus copy
- Proof of yellow fever vaccination, if required
- Extra glasses
- Electronics and chargers

Different issues arise regarding packing in terms of what you bring and the type of luggage you use. One tip, if you are traveling with your spouse and checking bags, is to consider dividing each person's things between the two checked bags in case one bag is delayed, then you each at least have some clothes.

- Will you check your bag or only bring carry-on? If you only bring carry-on, check on your airline's restrictions—airlines overseas may have different restrictions than US carriers. Some airlines only allow eight kilograms (17.6 lbs.) for your carry-on.
- How long are you going for?
- Where are you going to?
- What is the weather like?
- Will you need to bring special medication or mosquito repellent, most likely the kind with "deet?"
- What is the purpose of the trip—just fun, meetings, site visits, retreats, other?
- Are there any cultural restrictions on what you can wear?
- Will you be traveling through airports that are notorious for theft?

Some people pack the same amount of clothes no matter if they will be away for a week or a month. They will utilize the hotel laundry and/or hand-wash clothing. Others bring more clothes so that they have variety. A note about hotel or commercial laundries—while international hotel chains may handle your clothes with no problems, smaller or local hotels may be problematic. I know of one traveler who came home with all of his white clothes gray! You definitely do not want to have them clean very expensive items unless you are sure they will do a good job, or if you are desperate.

Where you travel to will also impact your decision on what to bring. Maybe you won't be staying in hotels, thus you may not have access to laundry service. Some countries may have laundromats or commercial laundries, but it depends on where you are. Or you may be on the move so much that every night will be in a different hotel, making it impossible to utilize the hotel's laundry service and a challenge for hand-washed clothes to dry.

Will the weather be hot, leading to lighter types of clothes, but maybe a need to change more frequently? Or will it be cold, requiring more layers of clothes? Also, remember to think about the seasons and where you are going. If you travel to the equator, it's always going to be hot, but if you are from the Northern Hemisphere and going to the Southern Hemisphere (or vice versa), the season is going to be the opposite of your home country. So, if you are going from Washington, DC to Mozambique in July, better take some sweaters with you, as it is winter in Mozambique. Do you want to pack long-sleeved shirts for a hot climate to protect your arms from the sun and mosquitoes?

If traveling for business, your industry will dictate the type of clothes you will need. Will it be formal, with business casual at nights? Is the entire trip casual because of the focus on field trips? Women find this more difficult and tend to need more types of clothes. It is easier for men to shed their coat and tie to look casual, but sometimes it is not so easy for women to do this.

Cultural norms in some parts of the world forbid wearing shorts, whether for men or women. Additionally, some places prohibit a woman from showing bare legs or arms. There are some best practice tips about what not to wear while traveling, such as not wearing revealing clothes in certain situations, including in churches or holy sites.[125] Buy a guidebook or research the location on the internet to prepare yourself and be appropriately dressed.

Lastly, some airports are notorious for theft. If you travel to or transit through such an airport, you may want to hand-carry your luggage (but check your airline's weight and size restrictions for carry-on luggage), or have your luggage shrink-wrapped (not a common thing in the US, but often available in other parts of the world).

WHAT TO BRING IN YOUR CARRY-ON LUGGAGE

Through my years of travel, I have figured out what is important to bring in my carry-on luggage in case I have to unexpectedly spend the night somewhere. For me, the most important items include an extra pair of underwear, a tooth-brush and toothpaste, a phone charger, and plug adapters. Since I often need multiple plug outlets, I also now carry a power strip with USB ports—this can come in handy if there are flight delays and limited electrical plugs in an airport. You will make new friends as people realize that you can help them charge their devices. Additionally, I carry some US dollars (including some small bills), at least two credit cards, and two ATM cards. Make sure you include your medications and an extra pair of eyeglasses. Some people also carry a change of clothing.[126]

I also hand-carry all my electronics and a photocopy of my passport and visas. Additionally, I bring my "cheat notes" that include all of the contact numbers and addresses I need,

---

125 "The 10 Worst Things to Wear While Traveling," *SmarterTravel* (blog), March 10, 2020.

126 Oskars Brumelis, "*75 Packing Tips for International Travel*," *CleverJourney* (blog), updated July 6, 2020.

such as for my hotel, the places I want to visit and restaurants I want to try, key words in the local language, and local tipping protocols. And lastly, I always carry a stash of food too!

And remember, currently you are only allowed to bring a quart-sized bag of liquids, aerosols, gels, creams, and pastes in your carry-on bag. These are limited to travel-sized containers that are 3.4 ounces or less per item. You can find a complete list of prohibited items at the US Department of Homeland Security, Transportation Security Administration's website.[127]

CUSTOMS

Your eligibility for a duty-free exemption when you return to the US, including the amount, depends on your residency status, the country you visited, and how long you were there.[128]

As of 2020, if you are a US resident returning from countries other than the Caribbean countries or US insular possession, you are entitled to an eight-hundred-dollar duty-free exemption and the next one thousand dollars' worth of goods you purchased is subject to a flat rate of 3 percent.[129]

OTHER THINGS TO KEEP IN MIND

Here are some miscellaneous tips that I always keep in mind:

---

127 US Department of Homeland Security, Transportation Security Administration, *What Can I Bring?*, accessed September 5, 2020.

128 US Department of Homeland Security, US Customs and Border Protection, *For USCitizens/Lawful Permanent Residents*, accessed September 5, 2020.

129 US Department of Homeland Security, US Customs and Border Protection, *Information Center*, accessed September 5, 2020.

- Make sure you charge all of your electrical devices before boarding your flight, although some airplanes, especially long-distance planes, now have USB ports on board.
- Electrical current: Check the electrical current at your destination. If it is different from your home country, you need to check to see if your electronics are dual voltage, otherwise you will need to bring a converter with you.
- Plug adapters: Do research online and check out what type of plugs are used—most of the time you will need to bring plug adapters. If you are traveling to multiple places, you can buy a multiple plug adapter, which often also contains a USB port too. Be careful of whether or not your plug has a ground—some plug adapters cannot accommodate a grounded plug. With the amount of electronic equipment that one brings with them now, you may need more than one plug adapter, and will also need to be aware that some hotels have a limited number of plug outlets. I now carry a power strip that is dual voltage and has USB ports as well.
- Make sure your mobile phone will work in the country you are going to, and check what the roaming charges may be.
- Medicines: Bring the normal medicines that you take plus any special medicine you may need, such as anti-malarial medicine, depending on where you are going. Mosquito repellent, especially with deet, may also be required. And don't forget the anti-diarrhea medicine.
- Bring a copy of your passport and your visas.
- Bring contact numbers for the place you are going to, including your hotel number.
- Bring a guidebook or a history book of the place you are visiting.

I hope that you are excited and are now more comfortable with traveling overseas. You will have so much fun on your new adventures! I would love to hear about them. Drop me a line at caroljyeeauthor@gmail.com.

ACKNOWLEDGEMENTS

I first wish to thank Professor Eric Koester and his Book Creators program, and also Lyn Solares for keeping us in line. Although I had been wanting to write a book for some time, it was through Eric's program that I wrote and published this book. I especially want to thank Elissa Graeser, my developmental editor, who helped me realize my dream. At New Degree Press, thanks go to Brian Bies and his team, including Jamie Tibasco, acquiring editor Max Abrams, and especially my marketing and revisions editor, Christy Mossburg.

I also want to thank those who allowed me to interview them and incorporate their stories into my book: Susan Puska, Gene Yee, Liz Kauffman, Barbara Fillip, Joanne Galloway, Owen Goslin, Alex Iseri, Nicole Lowery, Sanjiv Moré, Jane Lande Nick, Pete Siu, Brian Taussig-Lux, Dana Vierra, and Laura Gerdsen Widman.

And I wouldn't have been able to publish my book in its various media without my supporters who believed in my ability to write a book that I hope will make a difference: Indira Ahluwalia, Suzanne Alfaro, Maura Allen, Gwen Andersen, James Anderson, Darlene Faye Andrews, Konnie Andrews, Theresa Apple, Amy Atkinson, Kay Behrensmeyer,

Roula Baki Behrouzi, Jacob Bergsland, Kenzie Biggins, Molly Blasko, Amy Bodmann, Donald W. Boose, Jr., JoAnn Bowman, K David Boyer, Jr and Rebkha Atnafou, Eric Boyle, John Braun, Carla Briceno, Adam Brookes, Nancy Brown, Andrew Bryden, Jennifer Burdett, Melinda Burrell, Tony Butler-Sims, Anita Campion, Kevin Carroll, Deepika Chawla, Peggy Cho, Roshana Cohen, Donald Crane, Roni Crichton, Peggy Crockett, Susan DeLand, Isabel Delaney, Ray DeLong, Sherry Demaray, Dawne Deppe, Jenna Diallo, Debbie Driggers, Vicki Dunn, Elizabeth Ellis, Erin Endean, Kate Faust, Robert Flick, Amy Fox, Ken Gaalswyk, Nehal Gandhi, Moges Gebremedhin, Lisa Gihring, Michael Gold, Paul Guenette, Heidi Guest, Jean Hacken, Tamar Haddad, Elaine Haemisegger, Andy Hale, Devon Hardy, James Harris, Carolyn Wixson Hartwell, Kevin Haupt, Meredith Hedrick, Paul Hietanen, James Hochschwender, Oswaldo Holguin, Katie Horn, Elizabeth Hovey, Megan Huth, Linda Jarrett, Jaime Lee Jarvis, Beth Johnson, Sadete Kastrati, Liz Kauffman, Jay Kaufman, Bill Kedrock, Nancy Kim, Scott King, Justin Knepper, Scott Koepf, Eric Koester, Jan Lanzit, Franklin Lee, Gregory Lee, Ron Lee, Jeff Leone, Yolanda Lewis, Patrick Lohmeyer, Nicole Lowery, Caitlyn Lubas, Gene and Debbie Lum, Jessica Lum, Karen and Rodger Lum, Margaret Luttmann, John Lyon, David Mackey, Jennifer Mascardo, Sherry Mason, Michele McNabb, Read Admiral (retired) Eric McVadon and Marshall McVadon, Aaron Miller, Alicia Miller, Kathy Mitchell, Joanne Moore, Marcia Morgan, Bronwen Morrison, Cristina Mossi, Kevin Murphy, Marlene Murphy, Kristen Nelson, Kaylin B. Nickol, Amy Nielsen, Indeok Oak, Molly Ogro, Brian Oshea, Marianne Parente, Patrick Pearson, Erran Persley, Cecily Person, Janel Poche, Sarah Pogue, Timothy Prewitt, Jennifer Pruessner, William

Pulsipher, Jr., Susan Puska, Stephen Rahaim, Stacey Rasgado, Amy Regas, Linda Reynolds, Brennan Roy, Mollie Roy, Lloyd Ruona, Katherine Schad, David Schoolfield, Rebecca Sherwood, Kerry Sheu-Dong, Anne Simmons-Benton, Peter Siu, Laura Slattery, Anna Slother, Laura Smith, Shelley Spencer, Jacey Spratt, Brandon Stanley, Jeremy Strozer, Tina Thibault, Joseph Tolonen, Eugenio Torres, Nidia Trujillo, Tracy Trumbly, Matthew Tyson, John Ulshafer, Ai Victory, Ellie Vierra, Laura Vinoly, Raphael Vogelsperger, Judy Ward, Martin Webber, Laura Widman, Patricia Wilcox, Brenda Wilson, Colleen Parr Winans, Kathryn Wolf, Gwen Worley, Jocelyn Wyatt, Lilit Yoo, Bruce Yuke, Karen Zott, as well as those choosing to remain anonymous.

Lastly, I want to thank my fellow citizens of the world and all of the people I have met along the way. I am a richer person because of my interactions with you and look forward to new adventures in the future.

APPENDIX

INTRODUCTION

Blackall, Molly. "Global Tourism Hits Record Highs - but Who Goes Where on Holiday?" *The Guardian*, July 1, 2019. https://www.theguardian.com/news/2019/jul/01/global-tourism-hits-record-highs-but-who-goes-where-on-holiday.

Lane, Lea. "Percentage of Americans Who Never Traveled beyond the State Where They Were Born? a Surprise." *Forbes*, May 2, 2019. https://www.forbes.com/sites/lealane/2019/05/02/percentage-of-americans-who-never-traveled-beyond-the-state-where-they-were-born-a-surprise/#9a158492.

World Directory of Minorities and Indigenous Peoples. s.v. "Afghanistan: Pashtuns." Accessed August 27, 2020. https://minorityrights.org/minorities/pashtuns/.

CHAPTER 1

California Department of Parks and Recreation. "Immigration Station." Accessed August 27, 2020. https://www.parks.ca.gov /?page_id=1309.

History. "Chinese Exclusion Act." Updated September 13, 2019. https://www.history.com/topics/immigration/chinese-exclusion-act-1882.

Kath. "8 Jules Verne Quotes about Nature and Travel." *For Reading Addicts* (blog), February 8, 2016. http://forreadingaddicts. co.uk/authors/8-jules-verne-quotes-about-nature-travel/8774.

US Department of Commerce, US Bureau of the Census. *Historical Census Statistics on the Foreign-born Population of the United States: 1850-1990,* by Campbell Gibson and Emily Lennon. Population Division Working Paper No. 29. Washington, DC, February 1999. https://www.census.gov/history/pdf/1910foreignbornpop.pdf.

CHAPTER 2

AFS. *"Direct & Indirect Communication Styles."* Accessed August 28, 2020. https://www.afsusa.org/study-abroad/culture-trek/ culture-points/culture-points-direct-indirect-communication-styles/.

Anil. "English Language Statistics – an Exhaustive List." *Lemon Grad* (blog). Accessed August 28, 2020. https://lemongrad.com/ english-language-statistics/.

BrainyQuote. "Flora Lewis." Accessed August 28, 2020. https://www.brainyquote.com/quotes/flora_lewis_192058.

Ciolli, Chris. "10 English Words with Unfortunate Meanings in Other Languages." *AFAR*, February 2, 2017. https://www.afar.com/magazine/10-english-words-with-unfortunate-meanings-in-other-languages.

Dixon, Christine-Marie Liwag. "Baby Names That Mean Something Totally Inappropriate in Another Language." *The List* (blog), updated April 22, 2020. https://www.thelist.com/89031/baby-names-mean-something-totally-inappropriate-another-language/.

Korte, Gregory. "One-China Policy Gone Awry: White House Identifies XI as President of Wrong Country." *USA Today*, updated July 9, 2017. https://www.usatoday.com/story/news/politics/2017/07/08/white-house-identifies-xi-jinping-president-wrong-country/462068001/.

McWhorter, John. "The World's Most Musical Languages." *The Atlantic*, November 13, 2015. https://www.theatlantic.com/international/archive/2015/11/tonal-languages-linguistics-mandarin/415701/.

Naumann, Sara. "A Short History of Guangzhou." *TripSavvy* (blog), May 16, 2017. https://www.tripsavvy.com/short-history-of-guangzhou-1495124.

New World Encyclopedia. s.v. "Mao Zedong." Accessed August 28, 2020. https://www.newworldencyclopedia.org/entry/Mao_Zedong.

Nicole. "The 10 Most Common Languages." *Accredited Language Services* (blog). January 9, 2019. https://www.accreditedlanguage.com/languages/the-10-most-common-languages/.

Otte, T.G. Review of *Satow's Guide to Diplomatic Practice* by Sir Ivor Roberts, ed. *H-Diplo*, September 1, 2010. https://issforum.org/essays/PDF/Otte-Roberts.pdf.

Palmero, Luz. "How Learning a New Language Helps Brain Development." *Whitby* (blog). Accessed August 28, 2020. https://www.whitbyschool.org/passionforlearning/learning-a-new-language-helps-brain-development.

Randa A. "How Different Are Arabic Dialects." *Eton Institute* (blog), April 15, 2018. https://etoninstitute.com/blog/language/different-arabic-dialects.

Richards, Victoria. "Chart Shows 'What the British Say, What They Really Mean, and What Others Understand'." *Independent*, November 11, 2015. https://www.independent.co.uk/news/uk/home-news/chart-shows-what-british-people-say-what-they-really-mean-and-what-others-understand-a6730046.html.

Rodgers, Greg. "Saving Face and Losing Face." *TripSavvy* (blog), February 26, 2020. https://www.tripsavvy.com/saving-face-and-losing-face-1458303.

Sengupta, Durga M. "25 Indian Cities That Changed Their Names and What They Mean Now." *ScoopWhoop* (blog), November 11, 2014. https://www.scoopwhoop.com/news/whats-in-a-name/.

Siegelbaum, Lewis. "Baltic Independence." *Seventeen Moments in Soviet History* (blog). Accessed September 8, 2020. http://soviethistory.msu.edu/1991-2/baltic-independence/.

Southeastern University Online Learning. *"Intercultural Communication: High- and Low-Context Cultures."* August 18, 2016. https://online.seu.edu/articles/high-and-low-context-cultures/.

Telc Language Tests (blog). "5 Inspiring Quotes for Language Learners." January 2016. https://www.telc.net/en/about-telc/news/detail/5-inspiring-quotes-for-language-learners.html.

US Department of State, Office of the Historian. *The Collapse of the Soviet Union.* Accessed August 28, 2020. https://history.state.gov/milestones/1989-1992/collapse-soviet-union.

Wang, Hansi Lo. "Chinese-American Descendants Uncover Forged Family Histories." *CODE SW!TCH*, NPR, December 17, 2013. https://www.npr.org/sections/codeswitch/2013/12/17/251833652/chinese-american-descendants-uncover-forged-family-history.

CHAPTER 3

Akst, Jef. "The Influence of Soil on Immune Health." *The Scientist* (blog), January 8, 2020. https://www.the-scientist.com/news-opinion/the-influence-of-soil-on-human-health-66885.

Carman, Tim and Shelly Tan. "Made in America." *The Washington Post Voraciously,* October 11, 2019. https://www.washingtonpost.com/graphics/2019/voraciously/what-are-american-foods/.

Carr, Kelby. "Shop, Restaurant, and Museum Hours in France." *TripSavvy* (blog), updated June 11, 2019. https://www.tripsavvy.com/shop-restaurant-museum-hours-1516806.

Centers for Disease Control and Prevention. *Traveler's Health.* Accessed September 3, 2020. https://wwwnc.cdc.gov/travel/destinations/list/.

Center for Disease Control and Prevention (CDC). *Water, Sanitation, & Hygiene (WASH)-related Emergencies & Outbreaks: Making Water Safe in an Emergency.* Last reviewed February 24, 2020. https://www.cdc.gov/healthywater/emergency/making-water-safe.html.

Chili Pepper Madness (blog). "Homemade Curry Powder." June 19, 2019. https://www.chilipeppermadness.com/recipes/homemade-curry-powder/.

Devlin, Thomas Moore. "Why Is Sparkling Water All over Europe?" *Babbel Magazine* (blog), July 27, 2018. https://www.babbel.com/en/magazine/sparkling-water.

Gonzalez, David. "Guatemala Journal; Fried Chicken Takes Flight, Happily Nesting in US" *The New York Times*, September 20, 2002. https://www.nytimes.com/2002/09/20/world/guatemala-journal-fried-chicken-takes-flight-happily-nesting-in-us.html.

Guzman, Emily. "This Month in History: KFC Opens First Restaurant in China." *That's Shanghai* (blog), November 28, 2017. https://www.thatsmags.com/shanghai/post/21133/this-day-in-history-first-kfc-in-china.

Hoeller, Sophie-Claire. "How to Drink Espresso like an Italian." *Business Insider*, June 12, 2015. https://www.businessinsider. com/how-to-drink-espresso-like-an-italian-2015-6.

McElwain, Aoife. "Why Don't Americans Know How to Use a Knife and Fork?" *The Irish Times*, March 10, 2018. https://www. irishtimes.com/life-and-style/food-and-drink/why-don-t-americans-know-how-to-use-a-knife-and-fork-1.3409316.

Rodgers, Greg. "Chinese Table Manners: Basic Dining Etiquette." *TripSavvy* (blog), updated December 22, 2019. https://www. tripsavvy.com/chinese-table-manners-1458297.

Rodgers, Greg. "Table Manners and Food Etiquette in Thailand." *TripSavvy* (blog), updated February 26, 2020. https://www. tripsavvy.com/table-manners-in-thailand-1458507.

Ruggeri, Amanda. "15 International Food Etiquette Rules That Might Surprise You." *CNN Travel*, February 29, 2012. https://www.cnn.com/travel/article/international-food-eti-quette-rules/index.html.

TED Taste3 2008. "Jennifer 8. Lee: The Hunt for General Tso." July 2008. Video: 16:15. https://www.ted.com/talks/jennifer_8_lee_the_hunt_for_general_tso.

Thomson, Julie R. "The Most Famous and Greatest Food Quotes of All Time." *HuffPost*, updated December 6, 2017. https://www. huffpost.com/entry/food-quotes-famous-eating_n_2481583.

Teavivre (blog). "Traditional Chinese Tea Etiquette." Accessed August 29, 2020. https://www.teavivre.com/info/traditional-chinese-tea-etiquette.html.

UPB (blog). "The Story of Curry - and How It Became the UK's National Dish." April 14, 2016. http://upbproducts.co.uk/2016/04/14/story-curry-became-uks-national-dish/.

Wagner, Al B., Jr. "Food Technology & Processing: Bacterial Food Poisoning." *Texas A&M Agrilife Extension* (blog). Accessed August 29, 2020. https://aggie-horticulture.tamu.edu/food-technology/bacterial-food-poisoning/.

Wisti, Erin. "In Michigan, the Pasty Isn't X-Rated. It's a Portable Pie with History Baked in." *The Salt, NPR*, March 16, 2017. https://www.npr.org/sections/thesalt/2017/03/16/520129966/in-michigan-the-pasty-isnt-x-rated-its-a-portable-pie-with-history-baked-in.

CHAPTER 4

Bright Side (blog). "15 Hand Gestures That Have Different Meanings Overseas." Accessed August 26, 2020. https://brightside.me/wonder-places/15-hand-gestures-that-have-different-meanings-overseas-769110/.

Brooks, Richard. "Colours and Their Meanings around the World." *The Language Blog, K-International,* December 21, 2016. https://k-international.com/blog/color-meanings-around-the-world/.

Bulos, Nabih. "Saudi Women, Bucking Tradition, Forgo Abaya." *Los Angeles Times,* September 22, 2019. https://www.latimes.com/world-nation/story/2019-09-22/saudi-women-bucking-tradition-forgo-abaya.

Cultural Intelligence Center. "About Cultural Intelligence." Accessed August 26, 2020. https://culturalq.com/about-cultural-intelligence/.

Encyclopaedia Britannica Online. s.v. "Hong Kong." Accessed August 26, 2020. https://www.britannica.com/place/Hong-Kong.

Encyclopaedia Britannica Online. s.v. "Israel." Accessed August 26, 2020. https://www.britannica.com/place/Israel.

Gao, Helen. "How Did Women Fare in China's Communist Revolution?" *The New York Times,* September 25, 2017. https://www.nytimes.com/2017/09/25/opinion/women-china-communist-revolution.html.

Goodreads. "Stephen Cosgrove> Quotes." Accessed August 26, 2020. https://www.goodreads.com/author/quotes/35343.Stephen_Cosgrove.

History. "Palestine." Updated October 21, 2019. https://www.history.com/topics/middle-east/palestine.

Killian, Caitlin. "Why Do Muslim Women Wear a Hijab?" *The Conversation* (blog). January 15, 2019. https://theconversation.com/why-do-muslim-women-wear-a-hijab-109717.

Pant, Bhaskar. "Different Cultures See Deadlines Differently," *Harvard Business Review,* May 23, 2016. https://hbr.org/2016/05/different-cultures-see-deadlines-differently.

The World Clock – Worldwide. Accessed August 26, 2020. https://www.timeanddate.com/worldclock/.

UKEssays. "Effects of Globalization on Migration." November 26, 2018. https://www.ukessays.com/essays/cultural-studies/migration-in-the-era-of-globalization-cultural-studies-essay.php.

World Economic Forum. *Global Gender Gap Report 2020.* Cologny: World Economic Forum, 2019. http://www3.weforum.org/docs/WEF_GGGR_2020.pdf.

CHAPTER 5

Bonmatí, Damià S. "A Day in the Life of a Coyote: Smuggling Migrants from Mexico to the United States." *Univision*, December 21, 2016. https://www.univision.com/univision-news/immigration/a-day-in-the-life-of-a-coyote-smuggling-migrants-from-mexico-to-the-united-states.

Chaudhry, Suparna. "India's New Law May Leave Millions of Muslims without Citizenship." *The Washington Post*, December 13, 2019. https://www.washingtonpost.com/politics/2019/12/13/indias-new-law-may-leave-millions-muslims-without-citizenship/.

Cultural Intelligence Center. "About Cultural Intelligence." Accessed August 26, 2020. https://culturalq.com/about-cultural-intelligence/.

el-Komi, Ahmed. "Gaza's Christians Blocked from Travel to Bethlehem." *Al-Monitor*, December 24, 2018. https://www.al-monitor.com/pulse/originals/2018/12/palestine-israel-gaza-bethlehem-christmas-travel-permits.html.

Encyclopaedia Britannica Online. s.v. "South Africa." Accessed August 28, 2020. https://www.britannica.com/place/South-Africa.

Goodreads. "Mark Twain > Quotes > Quotable Quote." Accessed August 28, 2020. https://www.goodreads.com/quotes/1716-travel-is-fatal-to-prejudice-bigotry-and-narrow-mindedness-and-many.

International Labour Organization. "New ILO Figures Show 164 Million People Are Migrant Workers." Geneva: International Labour Organization, December 5, 2018. www.ilo.org/global/about-the-ilo/newsroom/news/WCMS_652106/lang--en/index.htm.

Martinez-Carter, Karina. "What Does 'American' Actually Mean?" *The Atlantic*, June 19, 2013. https://www.theatlantic.com/national/archive/2013/06/what-does-american-actually-mean/276999/.

Merriam-Webster Online. s.v. "What Is a 'Third-Culture Kid'?" Accessed August 28, 2020. https://www.merriam-webster.com/words-at-play/third-culture-kid.

Selth, Andrew and Adam Gallagher. "What's in a Name: Burma or Myanmar?" US Institute of Peace, June 21, 2018. https://www.usip.org/blog/2018/06/whats-name-burma-or-myanmar.

"Sunnis and Shia: Islam's Ancient Schism." *BBC*, January 4, 2016. https://www.bbc.com/news/world-middle-east-16047709.

TEDGlobal 2009. "Chimamanda Ngozi Adichie: The Danger of a Single Story." July 2009. Video, 18:34. https://www.ted.com/talks/chimamanda_ngozi_adichie_the_danger_of_a_single_story/transcript?language=en.

TEDxTrondheim. "Julien S. Bourrelle: How Culture Drives Behaviors." July 10, 2015. Video, 12:07. https://www.youtube.com/watch?v=l-Yy6poJ2zs.

The China Guide. "Chinese Ethnic Groups." Updated May 23, 2019. https://www.thechinaguide.com/blog/chinese-ethnic-groups.

Wise Old Sayings (blog). "Assumptions Sayings and Quotes." Accessed August 28, 2020. https://www.wiseoldsayings.com/assumptions-quotes/.

World Directory of Minorities and Indigenous Peoples. s.v. "Afghanistan." Accessed August 28, 2020. https://minorityrights.org/country/afghanistan/.

Worldometer (blog). "Nigeria Demographics." Accessed August 28, 2020. https://www.worldometers.info/demographics/nigeria-demographics/.

CHAPTER 6

Automotive News (blog). "SARS Spurs China Car Buying, but Tough Road Ahead." May 14, 2003. https://www.autonews.

com/article/20030514/REG/305140703/sars-spurs-china-car-buying-but-tough-road-ahead.

"China Has over 200 Million Private Cars." *Xinhuanet*, January 7, 2020. http://www.xinhuanet.com/english/2020-01/07/c_138685873.htm.

Fullerton, Jamie. "The Collector Using Classic Cars to Share the History of Communist China." *CNN Style*, updated January 18, 2017. https://www.cnn.com/style/article/china-classic-car-museum/index.html.

Greenberg, Andy. "A Guide to Getting past Customs with Your Digital Privacy Intact." Wired, February 12, 2017. https://www.wired.com/2017/02/guide-getting-past-customs-digital-privacy-intact/.

Lynkova, Darina. "How Fast Is Technology Growing Statistics." *Leftronic* (blog), updated May 2020. https://leftronic.com/how-fast-is-technology-growing-statistics/.

Mack, Lauren. "What Is a Mao Suit?" *ThoughtCo.* (blog). July 3, 2019. https://www.thoughtco.com/chinese-clothing-mao-suit-687372.

Phillips, Tom. "The Cultural Revolution: All You Need to Know about China's Political Convulsion." *The Guardian*, May 10, 2016. https://www.theguardian.com/world/2016/may/11/the-cultural-revolution-50-years-on-all-you-need-to-know-about-chinas-political-convulsion.

Railway Technology. "Beijing's Metro, Beijing Subway Development." Accessed August 31, 2020. https://www.railway-technology.com/projects/beijing_subway/.

Routley, Nick. "Meet China's 113 Cities with More Than One Million People." *Visual Capitalist*, February 6, 2020. https://www.visualcapitalist.com/chinas-113-cities-one-million-people-population/.

Sands, Lee M. "The 2008 Olympics' Impact on China." *China Business Review*, July 1, 2008. https://www.chinabusinessreview.com/the-2008-olympics-impact-on-china/.

Studwell, Joe. *The China Dream: The Quest for the Last Great Untapped Market on Earth.* New York: Grove Press, 2005.

University of Cambridge, Darwin Correspondence Project. "The Evolution of a Misquotation." Accessed August 31, 2020. https://www.darwinproject.ac.uk/people/about-darwin/six-things-darwin-never-said/evolution-misquotation.

Vocabulary.com Dictionary. s.v. "Ethnocentrism." Accessed August 31, 2020. https://www.vocabulary.com/dictionary/ethnocentrism.

Wong, Maggie Hiufu. "3 Billion Journeys: World's Biggest Human Migration Begins in China." *CNN Travel*, January 10, 2020. https://www.cnn.com/travel/article/chunyun-2020-lunar-new-year-travel-rush-china/index.html.

CHAPTER 7

Bye, Bente Lilja. "Volcanic Eruptions: Science and Risk Management." *Science 2.0*, May 27, 2011. https://www.science20.com/planetbye/volcanic_eruptions_science_and_risk_management-79456.

Centers for Disease Control and Prevention. *Traveler's Health.* Accessed September 3, 2020. https://wwwnc.cdc.gov/travel/destinations/list/.

Climate Signals beta. "Snowmageddon February 2010." Updated December 4, 2018. https://www.climatesignals.org/events/snowmageddon-february-2010.

Currencyfair (blog). "Tips on Gratuity: To Tip or Not to Tip around the World." January 3, 2017. https://www.currencyfair.com/de/blog/gratuity-to-tip-or-not-to-tip/.

Goodreads. "Epictetus > Quotes." Accessed September 3, 2020. https://www.goodreads.com/author/quotes/13852.Epictetus.

Goodreads. "Pico Iyer > Quotes." Accessed September 3, 2020. https://www.goodreads.com/author/quotes/75520.Pico_Iyer.

Horowitz, Jenny. "Tipping around the World: A Global Gratuity Guide." *Western Union\\WU* (blog). July 31, 2017. https://www.westernunion.com/blog/global-tipping-guide/.

Neale, Greg. "How an Icelandic Volcano Helped Spark the French Revolution." *The Guardian*, April 15, 2010. https://www.theguardian.com/world/2010/apr/15/iceland-volcano-weather-french-revolution.

United Nations World Tourism Organization (UNWTO). "Impact Assessment of the COVID-19 Outbreak on International Tourism." Updated May 2020. https://www.unwto.org/impact-assessment-of-the-covid-19-outbreak-on-international-tourism.

US Department of State, Bureau of Consular Affairs. *MyTravelGov.* Accessed September 3, 2020. https://travel.state.gov/content/travel.html.

US Department of State, Bureau of Consular Affairs. *Smart Traveler Enrollment Program (STEP).* Accessed September 3, 2020. https://travel.state.gov/content/travel/en/international-travel/before-you-go/step.html.

CHAPTER 8

Goodreads. "Maya Angelou > Quotes > Quotable Quote." Accessed September 5, 2020. https://www.goodreads.com/quotes/546179-perhaps-travel-cannot-prevent-bigotry-but-by-demonstrating-that-all.

Kvrgic, Dejan. "Fear of Travel: 11 Fears That Stop You from Traveling." *Lifehack* (blog). Accessed September 5, 2020. https://www.lifehack.org/272300/fear-travel-11-fears-that-stop-you-from-traveling.

PassItOn. "Oliver Wendell Holmes." Accessed September 5, 2020. https://www.passiton.com/inspirational-quotes/3586-a-mind-that-is-stretched-by-a-new-experience.

Szczepanski, Kallie. "What Was the Great Game?" *ThoughtCo.* (blog), July 31, 2019. https://www.thoughtco.com/what-was-the-great-game-195341.

"The 50 Best Travel Films of All Time." *Conde Nast Traveler,* March 16, 2020. https://www.cntraveler.com/galleries/2015-01-07/50-best-travel-films-of-the-past-50-years.

Williams, Amanda. "The World Is Not Safe – but You Should Explore It Anyway." *A Dangerous Business Travel Blog.* December 21, 2018. https://www.dangerous-business.com/travel-and-fear/.

FINAL THOUGHTS

Cultural Intelligence Center. "About Cultural Intelligence." Accessed August 26, 2020. https://culturalq.com/about-cultural-intelligence/.

Goodreads. "Kofi Annan> Quotes > Quotable Quote." Accessed September 5, 2020. https://www.goodreads.com/quotes/898533-we-may-have-different-religions-different-languages-different-colored-skin.

Peterson, Brooks. *Cultural Intelligence: A Guide to Working with People from Other Cultures.* Boston: Intercultural Press, 2004.

BONUS MATERIALS

Brumelis, Oskars. "*75 Packing Tips for International Travel.*" *CleverJourney* (blog). Updated July 6, 2020. https://www.cleverjourney.com/packing-tips-for-international-travel/.

Centers for Disease Control and Prevention. *Traveler's Health.* Accessed September 3, 2020. https://wwwnc.cdc.gov/travel/destinations/list/.

Perkins, Ed. "The 4 Different Types of Economy Airfare, Defined." *Airfarewatchdog* (blog). March 16, 2018. https://www.airfarewatchdog.com/blog/44251402/the-4-different-types-of-economy-airfare-defined/.

SmarterTravel (blog). "The 10 Worst Things to Wear While Traveling." March 10, 2020. https://www.smartertravel.com/10-things-never-wear-traveling-abroad/.

US Department of Homeland Security, Transportation Security Administration. *What Can I Bring?* Accessed September 5, 2020. https://www.tsa.gov/travel/security-screening/whatcanibring/all.

US Department of Homeland Security. *Trusted Traveler Programs.* Accessed September 5, 2020. https://ttp.dhs.gov/.

US Department of Homeland Security, US Customs and Border Protection. *For USCitizens/Lawful Permanent Residents.* Accessed September 5, 2020. https://www.cbp.gov/travel/us-citizens.

US Department of Homeland Security, US Customs and Border Protection. *Information Center.* Accessed September 5, 2020. https://help.cbp.gov/s/?language=en_US.

US Department of Homeland Security, US Customs and Border Protection. *Know Before You Go*. Accessed September 5, 2020. https://www.cbp.gov/travel/us-citizens/know-before-you-go.

US Department of State, Bureau of Consular Affairs. *MyTravelGov: International Travel*. Accessed September 3, 2020. https://travel.state.gov/content/travel/en/international-travel.html.

US Department of State, Bureau of Consular Affairs. *MyTravelGov: International Travel, Country Information*. Accessed September 5, 2020. https://travel.state.gov/content/travel/en/international-travel/International-Travel-Country-Information-Pages.html.

US Department of State, Bureau of Consular Affairs. *MyTravelGov: US Passports*. Accessed September 5, 2020. https://travel.state.gov/content/travel/en/passports.html/.